Surv2ved

No one noticed that while being STRONG, I was tired. I wasn't ok for years, and no one even knew.

by

Deneatrice Ledbetter

ISBN-978-1-960853-31-8

Liberation's Publishing LLC
West Point - Mississippi

Surv2ved

No one noticed that while being STRONG, I was tired. I wasn't ok for years, and no one even knew.

Table of Content

Thank Your Lord for all of your Intervention!

Chapter 1 *My Questions for you!*

Have you ever laid in bed at night, heart racing, chest tighten up, shortness of breath or feeling smothered? Has your face broken out like never before and no matter what cleanser or moisturizer you use it still gets worse due to stress? Have you ever stayed up 48 hours straight because you are scared to go to sleep due to you mind going one hundred miles per hour? Have you ever been that one sister, aunt, friend, cousin, co-worker that would come through to make things happen when others couldn't, and you worry yourself to death on HOW you can make things happen? Have you ever woken up in a good mood, and as soon as you walked out the door for work you become completely angry, and your anxiety goes through the roof, and you don't have a clue what triggered it? Have you ever had uncontrollably headaches and no matter what you took you still had no relief?

Have you ever been so stressed out that you had thoughts of ending it all, even attempting to end it? Have you ever experienced the loss of a loved one, and never seemed to get your life on track without them? Have you ever been the person who puts on the BIGGEST and FAKEST smile and when asked if you're okay, your reply is, "I'm fine." All the time you're about to break down right in front of them without them even knowing. Have you ever been the person who tries to keep everyone happy except yourself? Have you ever been the person who has always been there for someone no matter what they needed all for them to up and turn their back on you? Have you ever woken up in the middle of the night screaming JESUS, JESUS, JESUS, please help me? Have you ever looked in the mirror and asked, "why me?" Have you ever had someone tell you to get over losing someone because they are not coming back? Have you ever gone to the doctor's and been diagnosed with a million disorders and prescribed all kinds of meds just to keep your head level, but you refuse? If so, my last and final question is, DO YOU KNOW YOUR LORD AND SAVIOR JESUS CHRIST?

Never rush a person to heal, people deal with hurt, pain, and disappointment in many ways. Your way may not be the next person's way. What you may be able to handle the next person may not be able to handle so well. Instead of judging and talking down on a person, pray for them or with them, for healing. Be the kind of person to help another person heal. A simple text, phone call or even a visit could help a person more than you could imagine. You can never know what a person is going through if you've never encountered what they have experienced or what they went through. One day you can be on top of the world, and the next day the world can be on top of you, in the blink of an eye. So, never say what you could deal with when it has NEVER happened to you. Depression and STRESS is REAL, and a silent killer. #ButGOD

If you die today, the company you work for may call your family and give their condolences, they may even send a flower. But, within the next few days your job will be posted. They will replace you in a few days. People will make nice posts about you, go visit your family, and take them love offerings, rather its monetary, food, or prayers. Some will stand up at your funeral, and say kind words, as time passes people will stop calling/telling and the visits will STOP. Your loved ones you left behind will feel lost and only have the memories you shared with them. Take time for yourself. Make time for your family. Never go to bed angry, nor feel hurt. Fix what is wrong in any way you can. Take a vow to work on fixing anything that is wrong. Vow to be the bigger person and apologize first rather it's your fault or not. Don't be the person that wakes up to a call, or Facebook post, text, call, message saying "he or she gone' when you could have fixed or mend, the brokenness, before they left this world. One of my biggest flaws was holding, hurt, anger, secrets in to please others, and trying to handle a lot on my own due to pride. I didn't want to show weakness thinking I was so strong. If you are doing this STOP, it's a silent killer.

If you read book one, you should understand that after the rape, I was different, I was always angry and always offensive. I never told anyone, but I went into my aunt and uncle's closet because that's where I knew they kept their gun. I had plotted to go into their room that night to shoot and kill him for what he had done to me. I never went to therapy about it, nor talked about it. I dealt with it, and it was unfair because I was a young teenager. I was supposed to be protected not rapped by my uncle someone who was supposed to help raise me, tell me about how some boys are no good, and don't let them fool you to do something you don't want to do. But instead, he did the total opposite. I still feel he should be punished for what he did, but sometimes in life you must let the LORD fight your battles.

When I had my Ta'Dashea it taught me how to love and protect her from harm. I watched every person that met her and feared that something would happen to her like it did me. That's how I should have been protected. I needed to feel safe, and not alone.

* * *

Ta'Dashea Shardy Johnson, my first born, she was my smallest baby, of the three. She was basically a cheerleader throughout her years in school, even in college. She had a temper that makes me think back to my father. Make her mad she will fight a bull, no matter what the size. She also played softball, she loved the sport, and gave It her all. It was her 11th grade year in high school, she wanted to be in the beauty pageant at Starkville High. We got her this beautiful purple dress. She was beautiful! They called the third runners up name, then second, then first. My excitement had gone away, I just knew she would win one of those places, then then they said, "your Ms. Starkville High winner is Ta'Dashea Johnson," we all started screaming, with excitement. My beautiful baby had won the pageant. I never doubted her, but she was new to the school, and I just felt they wouldn't let her be the winner. I remember some of the parents in the crowd were so mad, but who gave a dam? I didn't think I was proud of my baby, and she was happy that's all that mattered. She never really gave me too many problems, like I gave my parents lol. She did things teenagers do, but nothing major, for the most part.

Ka'Daryal Mona Ledbetter my second daughter. She was my most athletic child. She had it in her blood line on my side and her father. She really didn't give me any issues when she got older, but when she was a child, she was bad as hell! She was a bully in her class, and she was mean af. When she started middle school, she toned things down a bit. That girl had me going to church having people laying hands on her she was so bad! Once she drove a guy's car in the ditch. I went to my mother's house to grab something, and I left her in the car with it running, because I was only going to be gone for a quick second. I came back outside, and the car wasn't under the carport anymore. I looked down the driveway and she was in the car upside down in the ditch laughing, she was three years old at the time. I had to find someone to get my car out of that ditch before the police drove by. You would have thought I had learned my lesson behind that =, but I didn't! I was nine months pregnant with my son, I went to the store to get me a coke, I'm still obsessed with cokes until this day. So, I left her in the car and went in the store, with the car running and her in it. I came back outside, and this girl was holding on to the steering wheels, showing all her pearly whites laughing! She had put the car in reverse and had backed all the way back into the gas pumps! She could have blown all our ass up! She almost put me in labor I was so mad. I thanked GOD daily when she grew out of being so bad.

Christopher LaShawn Harris Jr. My one and only son-shine was born on July 29, 1998, the last of my seeds. He was the most spoiled child of the three. He got anything he wanted from me and his dad and let's not leave out Perlisha and Charles, they had him rotten as well. He was the biggest crybaby you could have ever met. He hated school, and was a mama's boy, and STILL is. His second-grade year, Mrs. Hyde was his teacher he loved her so much, she broke him up from all that crying all the time she didn't play with him at all. She treated him like one of her own, she worked with him and got him where he needed to be without me lol. Chris favorite sport was baseball, he was good at it for the most. When we moved to Georgia, he was the star of his team. I didn't miss a game no matter what I had to do, it was just me and him. Bonnie and Clyde as they would call us. He is my protector still to this day. He has a heart of gold. It's a Blessing and a curse. He hates conflict and loves everyone to get along.

Chapter 2 *The Circle!*

It was so cold Christmas in 1980, and my sister Monique was just born the month before. I was sitting in front of the Christmas Tree. My eyes were so big from the excitement of the lights, and all the gifts under the tree. I couldn't wait to start opening my presents. My mom told me to wait for my dad to come downstairs before I started. When he finally came down, I opened the biggest one first. When I opened it, my eyes got even bigger. It was a pretty doll that was bigger than me! My mom said, "open your other gifts," while she was holding my sister in her arms. I smiled and said, "ok" and finished opening my gifts. I smelled the bacon coming from the kitchen. I think that's the reason I'm obsessed with bacon now. My mom cooked us a big Christmas breakfast. Bacon, eggs, rice, and some rolls. There isn't a person alive that can cook rice like my mother. I sat my doll in the chair beside me and asked my mom to fix her a plate too. My dad smiled, he could be nice, when he wanted to. My eyes have always been bigger than my belly, as older people used to say. After a few bites and eating up all the bacon I was full. I then went into my room and played with all the toys and my new doll, that I had named Annie. Where I got that from, I can't remember honestly. I played with my other toys.

Later that day, me and my dad went outside, and we played in the snow. It was so beautiful outside the snow covered the roads. And the mountains across the street. The snow almost came up to my knees. I had on a bubble coat that was bigger than me, lol, and some rain boots instead of snow boots. I had a skull hat on, with a few layers of clothes underneath. I had on so much stuff I could barely walk, all that gear was so heavy. My dad was the first person to show me how to make a snowball and make snow flurries. He made this big snowball, and I made one but just not as big. I threw mine at him, and then he threw his at me. When I say he threw it fast and as hard as he could, it almost knocked me off my feet. He hit me dead in the face. I ended up having a bruise on my left cheek. Keep in mind I was only five at the time.

We went into the house, and I whispered to my mom what he did. Keep in mind I was terrified of my dad, so that's why I was whispering. My, mom blurted out

"Charles why you hit her in her face like that, do you see this bruise?" My dad said "Shit, it's only a little snow, she will be alright!" He said it with no remorse, or nothing. My dad always made me feel like I was boy, the way he treated me. I just use to suck it up, hold my cries in, and wear a shield over my face to show I wasn't weak. My sister Monique was the highlight of most of my and my mom's days. Mom was a stay-at-home mother, and I would be at home with them in the summer. She would take us to the park that was located at the back of our apartments. I loved the swing set; it was my favorite. I got on the seesaw once and my slide hit the ground and tore my little pie up lol. It hit so hard I was too terrified to get on another one growing up. The playground seemed to be my mom's safe place. I would see her sitting on the bench in a daze at times, like she was lost in her thoughts. She would sometimes have this look on her face, that I can still see to this day when I think about her. Later I found out it was mostly about my dad. Remember everyone looked at Noah like a fool until it stared to rain...

I loved New Jersey, not just the cold weather and the snow. My mom seemed happy for the most part. My dad was stationed there after we left Columbus, Georgia, where I was born. I really don't remember too much about Georgia because I was young. New Jersey was where I started my first school and made friends for the first time. My mother was cool with the nosey neighbor lol. She knew everyone's business in the apartment complex. I used to hate to stay over there when my parents went out or had things to do. The smell in her house was horrible. Her furniture even smelled like old mold. When my mother came, pick us up our clothes and would smell just like her house. One morning my mother had to go to the grocery store, and we had to go over there. It was a Saturday morning, and I was watching cartoons. She gave me some cereal that had raisins in it. I ate the cereal and drunk the milk; I left the raisins in the bowl. She came in and asked why I had left the raisins. "I don't like them." was my reply. Next thing I know she came in back with a damn leather strap saying she was about to hit me across my back if I didn't eat them. I looked at her like she had went damn crazy. Then out of nowhere this woman wrapped me across my back. She hit me like twice. She was old and walked slumped over, with some nappy, matted up hair.

My first thought was to trip her ass up, but I know I would have really got a beat down by my dad when he got home. I took them licks and ate the raisins. I later found out the cereal was Rasin Brand, my grandmother Rosie Lee Ledbetter favorite cereal. After that incident I didn't want to go back over there. I still had to anytime my parents needed her to watch us.

Colorado was cold just like New Jersey for the most part in the wintertime. I liked it better there. My mother didn't have any friends there, but my father had friends on the base that he would hang out with, and sometimes they would come to the house, and drink. My father wasn't a drinker. He wouldn't drink, he was a smoker at that time. When my father's friends would come over my mother would make me go to my room and closed the door. I would either watch tv or play with my dolls, I had an obsession with dolls when I was little, I gave them all a name. Our apartment was so cozy and comfortable, but small. It wasn't as big as our townhouse in New Jersey, but I liked it more. The view was amazing, that's why I liked it so much.

When we moved to Colorado, things seemed to change. This was a little different. I'm guessing since I was a little older, I picked up on things that I had not at first. I began to understand what all the disagreements and arguments were about. I also, learned about all the affairs, drugs, and verbal abuse, that my mom was experiencing from my dad. My mom loved to cook when I was little. Her favorite thing to cook mostly was chicken and dumpling homemade of course. She would make sure that my dad had a hot plate when he got home, rather it was from work, or hanging out with his friends. My dad loved my mom's fried chicken. She would buy them whole and cut them up. My dad was the only one that could eat the legs. We were not allowed to ask for it. That was his part of the chicken. My mom was the BEST fried chicken person in the entire world. Whenever we had family functions, everyone wanted LAURA to fry the chicken. I don't know what she used to do to that chicken, but LORD have mercy it was good.

In Colorado, the schools were even different. The classrooms were large with a lot of children to one and sometimes two teachers. I didn't have many friends, it seemed like the kids that were in my classroom were closer because they lived by each other, or parents were friends. I was basically a new kid on the block, so I felt like a loner at times, but eventually I was perfectly fine with it.

The time came for us to move to my dad's hometown, good ole Mississippi. My mom was ready to go. We sold everything we had for the most and packed our clothes and drove back to the place where my mom and dad knew as home. My cousin LaToya, who was my dad's sister's child, was my very first best friend. Toya was on the quiet side for the most, until you made her mad. Her mom was Linda Weatherby. Her husband was Sanders Weatherby, but we called him uncle Snake. My aunt Linda used to always tell me all the time "Dee you the only one who can get Toya well when she's sick." Everyone called me the fun, but bad ass cousin lol. When Toya moved to Atlanta that hurt me. I told her all my secrets and she was the one who would try to get me out of trouble. It would be so funny. Family would say, "stop lying for Dee!" One time I told her about this boy I was going to hook her up with. I told her he had green eyes light skinned and was tall. She would write letters and give them to me to give to him lol. Keep in mind she had never seen him before lol. She was furious with me when she found out who it was! When she finally seen him the ONLY thing that was green about him was his last name! Man, we laugh about that to this day.

Toya was quiet, nothing like me. I used to call her sneaky. She left me to do 7th grade by myself. She was all I knew as a friend. Attending Hunt School without my first best friend/cousin was a big change for me. But I went and made it do what it do. I met new friends, and I'm still friends with most until this day. I was a fighter, and a class clown. Once I got into a fight with one of my friends about a damn Snicker's bar. I got mad because we were supposed to split it, but when she broke it, she gave me the small piece. I got mad and was ready to fight.

Back then they were only fifty cents, but it was hard to even get a dollar back then. Money was tight as well as hard times every dollar counted. The principal called my mother and told her I had got into a fight and to come and get me. I was suspended for three days. My mother was furious. My father beat my ass and made me clean the entire three days I was suspended. He had me wash walls, and base boards. My father is the reason I have OCD now.

They announced we were having a talent show, boy I had got excited, because Mrs. Chism, the music teacher at Mitchell Memorial School, had fooled me like I could sing. So, I signed up. I signed up to sing, "Here and Now" by Luther Vandross.

They called my name, and it was my turn to show what I had. I took a breath and began to sing.

One look in your eyes and there I see
Just what you mean to me
Here in my heart I believe
Your love is all I'll ever need
Holdin' you close through the night
I need you, yeah
I look in your eyes and there I see
What happiness really means
The love that we share makes life so sweet
Together we'll always be
This pledge of love feels so right
And, ooh, I need you
Here and now
I promise to love faithfully (Faithfully)
You're all I need
Here and now
I vow to be one with thee (You and me), hey
Your love is all (I need) I need
Say, yeah, yeah
When I look in your eyes, there I'll see
All that a love should really be
And I need you more and more each day
Nothin' can take your love away
More than I dare to dream
I need you
Here and now
I promise to love faithfully (Faithfully)
You're all I need

Here and now
I vow to be one with thee (You and me), yeah
Your love is all I need
Ooh, and I'm starting now
I believe (I believe in love), I believe
(Starting here) I'm starting right here
(Starting now) Right now because I believe in your love
So I'm glad to take the vow
Here and now, oh
I promise to love faithfully (Faithfully)
You're all I need
Here and now, yeah
I vow to be one with thee (You and me), yeah
Your love is all I need........

My eyes were closed majority of the time, for one because I was kind of ashamed, and for two when you close your eyes to sing, it helps with confidence. My classmates cheered, and some laughed the entire time because they couldn't believe I sang in front of the entire school.

In the summer, my mom would send me, Monique and Narquita to the country in Brooksville Mississippi, where she was originally from. I used to hate it because there was absolutely nothing to do. My cousin Perlisha became my best friend. We were first cousins, she was my mom's niece, my mom's brother Frank child, we are the same age so that's why we were the closet. She had an older brother, Dewayne, and a baby sister, Rena. She had some more sisters and brothers on her dad's side, but I didn't know them. Her mom's name is Ethel, LORD that woman could cook especially chicken and dressing. Until this day, I pay her at thanksgiving time to make me a pan. She had an aunt named Mary that I thought was the prettiest lady ever. Me and Lisha did some stuff. She introduced me to some of her friends, The Brewers. The Brewers stayed by Pilgrim Rest church and on 388. So, her friends I consider my friends. Keisha, Annie ruth, Mary Ann, just to name a few. Then it was Nesha and Boo, which I called extended family that we would hang out with. Our family lived in what I called, "The Circle."

Our cousin Laura was the first house you came to when you came to the little subdivision. My mom was her favorite. She gave her the nickname Nuge. She had plum trees. I had a tree that was specifically for me. It was an apricot tree; it had the biggest plums I've ever seen in real life. When I got pregnant later, she would not let me get on her trees. She said I would kill the tree because I was pregnant. Her house was extremely old, she had a beautiful picture of my mom hanging on her wall in her living room. I used to beg her for that picture, but she would never give it to me. The house had a kitchen, two bedrooms, but no bathroom. She would have to use the bathroom outside in an outhouse she had. She didn't have running water either. She would come down to my grandmother's house to get jugs of water at a time. We would help her sometimes. I wholeheartedly loved her. She was real and uncut reminded me so much of myself. She spoke her mind and didn't care who didn't like it. Some people called her a witch. They said she was so evil, but I had never seen that side of her. When she passed her funeral was mysterious. A very dark cloud came over the church and it started storming. The sky had literally fallen out of the sky. That's what we used to say when it starts storming badly. Everyone in the church started looking with fear on their faces. It was a scary feeling. I was thinking to myself she about to come back and get ya'll ass lol. I'll never forget that day.

The next house in The Circle was my uncle Limp, and aunt Nita's house. They had three children Shirley, Bobbie, and Leshone who are my first cousins. Shone was the one around my age, so me him, Lisha and Wayne were the tightest. One time we were at my grandmother's house eating Sunday dinner on the 3rd Sunday. That was big for us. We would leave church, then have feast for dinner. Me and Shone were out by the gas tanks playing with rocks. A truck came driving past and we squatted down and threw rocks at it. The guy jumped out of the truck and started cussing at us. My uncle Limp seen it from afar. We took off running to the house and we both ran to our mothers. My uncle had a green rubber hose. He grabbed both of us, took us outside and made us lay across the gas tank and tore our asses up. He didn't play and we all were so scared of him. I learned my lesson that day to NOT throw rocks at people's cars. I was bad as hell.

My uncle drove a van and took workers to work at Sanderson Plumbing. That's how we mostly got to my grandmother's house in the summer. One day while on the van my sister Monique said, "Junior driving this van so got damn fast." Everyone on the van died laughing they were so tickled, but she was scared she was going to get in trouble for cussing. My uncle Limp nickname was Junior, that's what we called him. Block, who was a close family friend that was on the van that day would joke about it even after we got grown.

The next house was my grandmother's house. That's where me and my sisters stayed most when we went down south every summer. My grandmother would cook the best homecooked meals ever. She and my uncle Frank would plant their crop every year. Once the chickens were in the garden scratching the seeds up. My grandmother would have us chase all the chickens to the outhouse. She had an ax and would chop their toenails off. That scared me to death. My grandmother wasn't scared of anything lol. I think I got a little of that from her also. On Saturdays, we would go to town, and go to Tem's grocery store. We would get "Stage Planks" as she called them. They were ten for a dollar. I loved the ones with the pink icing on them. Food was much cheaper back then, but we mostly ate out of the garden. My grandmother was super tight with the Mennonites. She would buy stuff from them often. I think my grandfather had a relationship with them before he passed. My family use to tell use he was a POWERFUL man, and what he said goes. I never met him, but I heard a lot of things about him. I heard he was mean and lowdown, (kind of put me in the mind of my father, when I heard the stories about him). One story that stuck with us all was how he used to bury money out in the field behind the house. We would go out there and dig looking for money lol. I was praying one day I would find at least one of those gold coins. My grandparents owned a lot of land down there, I was told that my grandfather 'gifted" Pilgrim Rest church some land, and that's where the cemetery is to this day.

The nest and final house were where my uncle Frank, aunt Ethel, and my cousins, Lisha, Wayne, and Rena stayed. Lisha's mom showed her how to cook at an early age. She could throw down at the age of twelve in the kitchen. She would have a whole hot meal ready by the time her mom got off every day. The things we used to do while her parents were at work, I dare NOT to tell lol. We would get beaten at our age now and we are almost 50!

One summer the Noxubee School District, let children in other districts attend their summer school program. I was so happy because there was nothing to do down there in the summertime. I couldn't wait to get on that bus. When the guys there saw me, they were asking my cousins who I was and where I was from. I flirted with a few of them, but nothing serious. It was one that stood out from the rest, we talked, but he had a girlfriend, and that girl was crazy like those people on lifetime no lie. He told me they had broken up, but she wasn't having that. So, to help keep her sanity., I didn't talk to him. After that experience I had made a vow to NEVER talk nor date a guy from Noxubee County ever! But, many years later I did and whew is all I can say lol.

September 25, 1990, all of us were in bed asleep. We woke up the next day to find out that a little three-year-old daughter of the family that was staying in my uncle and aunt's house was missing. Everyone was devastated. Everyone wanted answers. How could a three-year-old be missing in a small town of only family? The police and detectives went house to house questioning my entire family. They even took two of my family members down for questioning and tried to frighten them to confess to something they didn't do! It was a nightmare. Family and friends gathered to help search for the missing little girl, it was so sad. She was finally found in a pond within walking distance from the house dead. We could not believe it. They ended up charging the mother's boyfriend for the rape and murder. They sentenced him to prison for something that he didn't do. They threw that man life away for lack of evidence, just to find out he didn't do it and another man confused.

Brewer was convicted of capital murder and sent to death row. He spent 16 years in Parchman. Just as Brooks had done, Brewer proclaimed his innocence throughout. In 2001, DNA tests proved Brooks was not the killer and his conviction was overturned. You ever heard of the wrong place at the wrong time? This sometimes can be a fact. A man that gave almost 20 years of his life to the system for a crime he didn't commit. He can never get those years back. When all this took place, I was fourteen years ole.

It was 1991 "Naughty by Nature" came out with a song OPP, if you know you know. It was one of my favorite songs. I would bust a beat then I would start rapping:

OPP, how can I explain it
I'll take you frame by frame it
To have y'all jumping' shall we singing' it
O is for Other, P is for People scratching' temple
The last P... well... that's not that simple
It's sort of like another way to call a cat a kitten
It's five little letters that are missing' here
You get on occasion at the other party
As a game 'n it seems I got to start to explain'
Bust it

You ever had a girl and met her on a nice hello

You get her name and number and then you feeling' real mellow
You get home, wait a day, she's what you want to know about
Then you call up and it's her girlfriend or her cousin's house
It's not a front, F to the R to the O to the N to the T
It's just her boyfriend's at her house (Boy, that's what is scary)
It's OPP, time other people's what you get it
There's no room for relationship there's just room to hit it
How many brothers out there know just what I'm getting' at
Who thinks it's wrong 'cos I'm splitting' and co-hitting' at
Well if you do, that's OPP and you're not down with it
But if you don't, here's your membership

You down with OPP (Yeah you know me), you down with OPP (Yeah you know me)
You down with OPP (Yeah you know me), who's down with OPP (Every last homie)
You down with OPP (Yeah you know me), you down with OPP (Yeah you know me)
You down with OPP (Yeah you know me), who's down with OPP (All the homies)

Also, I absolutely love LL COOL J song 'I Need Love" it came out in 1987, but I didn't start liking it until 1991 when I THOUGHT I was in love lol. I knew the entire song by heart, I wrote down the song on notebook paper and learned it word for word. I would lay in my bed and stare at the wall like the lyrics said and then I would sing:

When I'm alone in my room sometimes I stare at the wall
And in the back of my mind I hear my conscience call
Telling me I need a girl who's as sweet as a dove
For the first time in my life, I see I need love.

There I was giggling about the games
That I had played with many hearts, and I'm not saying no names
Then the thought occurred, tear drops made my eyes burn
As I said to myself, "Look what you've done to her".

I can feel it inside, I can't explain how it feels
All I know is that I'll never dish another raw deal
Playing make believe pretending that I'm true
Holding in my laugh as I say that I love you.

Surv2ved

Saying, "Amor", kissing you on the ear
Whispering, "I love you and I'll always be here"
Although I often reminisce, I can't believe that I found
A desire for true love floating around.

Inside my soul because my soul is cold
One half of me deserves to be this way 'til I'm old
But the other half needs affection and joy
And the warmth that is created by a girl and a boy

I need love.

I need love.

Romance, sheer delight, how sweet?
I got to find me a girl to make my life complete
You can scratch my back, we'll get cozy and huddle
I'll lay down my jacket so you can walk over a puddle
I'll give you a rose, pull out your chair before we eat
Kiss you on the cheek and say, "Ooh girl, you're so sweet"
It's déjà vu whenever I'm with you
I could go on forever telling you what I do

But where are you at? You're neither here nor there
I swear I can't find you anywhere
Damn sure you am not in my closet, or under my rug
This love search is really making me bug
And if you know who you are why don't you make yourself seen?
Take the chance with my love and you'll find out what I mean
Fantasies can run, but they can't hide
And when I find you I'm pour all my love inside

I need love.

I need love.

I want to kiss you, hold you, never scold, you just love you
Suck on you neck, caress you and rub you
Grind, moan and never be alone
If you're not standing next to me, you're on the phone
Can't you hear it in my voice? I need love bad
I got money, but love's something I've never had
I need your ruby red lips sweet face and all
I love you more than a man who's 10 feet tall.

I'd watch the sunrise in your eyes
We're so in love when we hug we become paralyzed
Our bodies explode in ecstasy unreal

Deneatrice Ledbetter

You're as soft as a pillow and I'm as hard as steel
It's like a dream land, I can't lie, I never been there
Maybe this is an experience that me and you can share
Clean and unsoiled yet sweaty and wet
I swear to you this is something I'll never forget

I need love.

I need love.

See what I mean? I've changed, I'm no longer
A playboy on the run, I need something that's stronger
Friendship, trust, honor, respect, admiration
This whole experience has been such a revelation
It's taught me love and how to be a real man
To always be considerate and do all I can
Protect you, you're my lady and you mean so much
My body tingles all over from the slightest touch

Of your hand and understand I'll be frozen in time
'til we meet face to face and you tell me you're mine
If I find you, girl, I swear I'll be a good man
I'm not going to leave it in destiny's hands
I can't sit and wait for my princess to arrive
I got to struggle and fight to keep my dream alive
I'll search the whole world for that special girl
When I finally find you watch our love unfurl
I need love

I need love.

Girl, listen to me

When I be sitting in my room all alone, staring at the wall
Fantasies, they go through my mind, and
I've come to realize that I need true love
And if you want to give it to me, girl, make yourself seen
I'll be waiting
I love you.

That was my shit! His lips made you want to do something. Especially when he licked them lips, a bitch got wet by the thought of it lol.

Chapter 3 *Look at you now!*

I lived next door to Mrs. Gardner and Brady starting my 9th grade year. Me and Brandy became good friends. Her cousin Terylinn became one of my good friends as well. We hung out at each other's houses. Practice dance routines together, you name it, we did as teenagers.

We were the first class to start at Lee high for the 9th and 10th grade. They had converted the schools together. The 11th and 12th grade was at Caldwell. The school colors changed from red and white to purple and gold, we were officially Falcons! The new high school brought a lot of people together and it helped people to get along better. When the schools were divided it caused hate, and animosity in me anyway. I've learned that once you get to learn and know a person for yourself that's when you really can get your own personal thoughts about a person. Listening to others sometimes can mess up some of the best parts of your life. You can miss out on good people. I've also learned you must have the energy you want to attract. That cloud you have over your head today can be the water you drink tomorrow once it starts to rain remember that. Learn to love the rain, it doesn't stop anything but a drought! Learn to be a go-giver instead of a go-getter all the time, find your PEACE. It's ok to put up a wall sometimes, not to block anyone out, but to see who cares enough to climb over it to see if you are ok. Until you change your way of thinking, you will recycle your experiences. And always remember wounds can turn into weapons to help you fight off evil spirits, and people.

In my voice, "if you don't want to grow you got to go."

When I changed schools in the 10th grade and went to West Lowndes High School, things started to get better. Wendy was my road dog. We used to be on our necks pregnant and all. We walked, took taxis, drove our mothers' cars, anywhere we wanted to go. Her sister Nookie had a house on northside where we would stay sometimes. It was a hangout spot. Me and Wendy loved our DuckHead™, Girbaud™, Ivy Crew™, Guess™, Tommy Hilfiger™, K-Swiss™ and Nikes™, just to name a few. We wore our clothes big. I guess because we were so little. I tried out for the basketball team; Ms. Jane Coleman was the basketball coach at the time. My dad was an awesome basketball and baseball player. My sisters

Monique and Narquita took after my dad. Me on the other hand I didn't. My mind was somewhere else, not on basketball, I was horrible at it. The only reason I tried it out was so that I could be on the bus with Shawn. He was on the boys' basketball team.

Ms. Coleman only reason for letting me on the team was because of my height, and she knew my dad was a beast at basketball. Once my daddy came to see me play. I'll never forget what he said, "why you went out there and made a fool of me." We all laughed because that's exactly what I did, made a fool of myself. I could rebound Tho because I was so aggressive. If my dad had taken time up with me and my sisters, I feel we would have been unstoppable in any sport, because he was an awesome athlete. He won so many awards and had a scholarship to Rust Community College for basketball. He also could run extremely fast. He was basically an all-around guy for the most.

Once me and Wendy, went to Snooty Fox both of us was pregnant. It was a club in the plaza on highway 82. We danced and partied that night like we weren't even pregnant. I got home that night and was hurting so bad, went to the emergency room thinking I was having contractions, but it was only false labor. They kept me overnight for observation, but they sent my ass home the next morning. My mom told me "Dee it's time for you and Wendy to sit ya'll asses down somewhere. Going to these clubs partying like you don't have a whole baby in your stomach." My mom told me when she found out I was pregnant that I did it on purpose because Wendy and another friend that hung out with us were pregnant. All three of us were pregnant at the same time. All our children were born the same year a few months apart. We were the pregnant pack lol. I was on my second one. My oldest I had at sixteen. And here I was pregnant again, at the age of nineteen. People used to judge me, saying that I had two children before I was twenty years old. I never once let that bother me or stop me. I kept my head held high and walked with pride. I was still in school and working. My mom was my backbone. I still did everything I wanted to do in life. Having children early didn't stop me from doing absolutely anything!

In life remember just, because you do things out of, 'MAN ORDER" doesn't mean what you did is wrong.

Life is what you make of it. I had my children young, then got married, then finished school. Who's to say that the order I put it in was wrong. Some people I know did it in the order they thought was right and are now living miserable. If GOD is not the head of your life, no matter what order it's in you will not blossom into all what HE has in store for you. Yes, he may give it to you, but can you keep it? Can you manage it without him? Can you be faithful unto HIM? Never let a soul tell you what you can't do or have in life. Never let a soul tell you that you can't change, no matter how late in life you try to get it right, as long as you get it right. It's no timeframe for getting it right. When judgment day comes, HE will ask you about your sins, not the next person, you must be accountable for what you do. Life is not easy, and life is not hard, it's what you make out of it.

It was summer 1996, it was hot, but not like the heat is now. The heat now is dangerous it will kill someone if you are out in it too long. We were at my mom's house on 11th Ave on the south side when my light-up phone rang. It was red with all the flashing lights in the background. It was one of my friends. They said, "Dee Shawn, has another girl at the baseball field while he's at practice." Keep in mind, I had the mindset that I could whip anyone including him! I got into my mom's car and went to West Lowndes baseball field. Coach Green was the coach at the time. He knew about me and Shawn, so as soon as he saw me, he immediately told me to leave. I had Booty on my side walking to the field. First, I stopped and looked at the girl, snapped out on her so badly that she got in her car and left. Then, I was headed straight to the field to get his ass. Got to the field and we started fussing, all his friends were just shaking their heads, because this was routine for us, always fussing and fighting. He told me "If you didn't have my baby in your hands, I would knock your ass out." Guess what I did? I put her down on the ground and said now hit me. Let's just say he tore my ass up, for one for putting Booty on the ground, and for two he was sick of my mouth. That night he came over and we made up like nothing happened. That too was like a routine for us. One thing I can say is he sure did show me how to fight lol.

It's not ok for anyone man or woman to put their hands on you. If it ever gets that bad, walk away and leave. Abuse is never ok verbally, or physically. It can scar you for life and it have you dealing with issues for the rest of your life. You are good enough. Anything that you are battling for in life you can overcome. That relationship that ended and you felt you couldn't move on without them, look at you now. That job that let you go and probably wasn't treating you right, look at you now. Succeeding rather its more pay or less pay. That child that just won't listen, take it to LORD, give it to HIM, and watch how HE turn things around for the best. The best may not be what you want it to be. Remember HE knows what's best. Never dim your light to make others feel comfortable. Ask yourself, would they dim theirs? Just because their house is bigger than yours, is it a home? Their cars are luxury cars, but you have a car that has air, heat, tires, and a good motor, and gets you to everywhere you need to go just fine. Don't be jealous because you have no clue what they are going through or how hard they must work just to afford that luxury car. The designer is just that designer. It doesn't define who you are or aren't. In the words of my late aunt Bernice, "whatever floats your boat!"

Deneatrice Ledbetter

Chapter 4 *A Day in the Life!*

It was 1997 there I was with two children, Ta'Dashea and Ka'Daryal, going to school, working at Taco Bell™, and still trying to be a teenager. In the mist of being a mother to my two girls, my mom had my back. My support system was unreal. Dashea was this big-bright eyed living doll. My mother, aunt Nancy, and cousin Perlisha had her rotten. As, for Ka'Daryal her father side, his siter Jenny, and his mother Gloria, helped with her like she was their own. I never had to worry about a babysitter because Jenny always had her. I would sometimes stay down there at her house with them because she treated me like family. They still do to this day. Her girls Shomika, and Toya were my little nieces, they still are to this day. When I moved into my own apartment they would come and stay with me sometimes.

Every summer in Artesia they would play baseball. We all would go out there to support our friends. Sometimes it would be two or three girlfriends, to one guy. It's funny now that I look back on it, but back then, it was hurtful to some of those girls. But if we felt like we were the "main girl" we didn't care about the others. Some of the girls would look so stupid but didn't care as long as they got their time with them when the "main girl" left. Standards were low just to say that they were dating someone, in the "popular crowd." Girls were doing anything and everything to win first place in a guy's life, to only get a baby out the deal, hurt, or embarrassed. As we got older, we realized how much of a precious jewel we really were. In my mother's voice "sometimes bought lessons, are the best lessons." We live and we most defiantly learn.

I used to get mocked especially by teachers, family, and some friends, about having two daughters at the age of 19. I even had one teacher at Columbus High to tell me that I was damaged goods, in so many words. But little did they know that I was beyond good. I see that teacher from time to time, and I look at her, so many times I wanted to walk up to her and, say, "Look at me! Look at who you basically gave up on and said would be a single mother with no help." But she looks so unhappy, alone, and to be honest doesn't even take care of herself. You must be careful about putting your mouth on people and their children. KARMA is real, and if you don't believe in it, please believe GOD is real!

On Sundays we used to hang out on 20th Street, around Hunt jr. High. Bills Drive-In was across the street and the park. Everyone made sure they were ready for Sundays. We would have our outfits, hair, and lip gloss shining just to get on northside lol. The guys would come through with their cars, and loud music, blunts smoke all through the air. Guys asking their friends to let them get the shorts on that cigarette. Man, the times we had, good, clean, fun. It was no mess, no hating, no jealousy, no fighting, no backstabbing, no nothing for the most. Every now and then it would be a fight, or disagreement but nothing major. We would sit out there until nightfall. The police wouldn't even bother us or make us leave, as long as it was peaceful, with no drama.

Once, my daughter's father paged me and I went across the street to call him back on the payphone. He asked where I was, and I lied and said down the street from my mom's house. We hung up and a few minutes later he walked up to me, asking why I lied. I couldn't even part my lips to say anything. When he walked up, I was smiling and grinning in another guy's face. That day he broke up with me. I went home and cried, and played one of my favorite songs, that we all played when we were broken hearted by a guy back then, My girl Mary J. Blige. Back then sending your mate, lyrics to a song when things wasn't going right fixed everything seem like lol. I sent him a long text message with every word of the lyrics, while tears ran down my face as I typed:

> While all the time that I was loving you
> You were busy loving yourself
> I would stop breathing if you told me to
> Now you're busy loving someone else
> Eleven years out of my life
> Besides the kids, I have nothing to show
> Wasted my years, a fool of a wife
> I should have left your ass long time ago
> Well, I'm not gon' cry
> I'm not gon' cry
> I'm not gon' shed no tears
> No I'm not gon' cry
> It's not the time
> 'Cause you're not worth my tears
> I was your lover and your secretary
> Working every day of the week
> Was at the job when no one else was there
> Helping you get on your feet
> Eleven years of sacrifice
> And you can leave me at the drop of a dime
> Swallowed my fears, stood by your side
> I should've left your ass a thousand times
> Well I'm not gon' cry
> I'm not gon' cry
> I'm not gon' shed no tears
> No I'm not gon' cry
> It's not the time
> 'Cause you're not worth my tears
> I know there are no guarantees
> In love you take your chances
> But somehow it seems unfair to me
> Look at the circumstances

Through sickness and health
'Til death do us part
Those were the words that we said from our heart
So now when you say that you're leaving me
I don't get that part
 I was your lover and your secretary
Working every day of the week
Was at the job when no one else was there
Helping you get on your feet
Eleven years of sacrifice
And you can leave me at the drop of a dime
Swallowed my fears, stood by your side
I should've left your ass a thousand times
 Well I'm not gon' cry
I'm not gon' cry
I'm not gon' shed no tears
No I'm not gon' cry
It's not the time
'Cause you were never worth my tears
 Well I'm not gon' cry
I'm not gon' cry
I'm not gon' shed no tears
No I'm not gon' cry
It's not the time
'Cause you were never worth my tears
 Well I'm not gon' cry
I'm not gon' cry
I'm not gon' shed no tears...

We ended up getting back together but, it didn't last too much longer after that lol.

* * *

I was 20 years old with two children. Dashea and Booy (the nickname her dad gave her). Moved into my first apartment. It was in Applewood down 69 right behind Yorkville apartments. I had my apartment fully furnished. I had gone to this furniture store and started me some credit knowing damn well I really couldn't afford, that high bill. I bought a kitchen set, a living room, and a stereo system, bunkbeds, and me a four-piece bedroom set. The stereo I had was so loud the entire complex could hear it. Once I cut it on, they knew it was me. Tab was my downstairs neighbor we were super cool, so she didn't mind when I played it. The girl that lived next door to me was in a relationship with my oldest daughter's father. Honestly, I didn't give a damn about what they had going on because I was in love with Shawn, Booty's dad. She would make a scene when he would come over to her house.

Once I was locking my door to leave for work and she opened her door and stopped me. She said, "Dee do you have a problem with me." I've always been a hothead, I said "Do it look like I got a problem with you? "Bitch who are you?" She then goes to say, "I'm just asking because you don't speak." I told her "I've been living beside you for almost two years, and BEFORE you even started screwing my baby daddy, hell I wasn't speaking to you then!" I then walked my skinny ass off got in my car and went to work. I really wanted to kick her ass, but then I would have been late for work lol. One thing you don't do is approach me about a no man! If you are that insecure, re-evaluate yourself.

* * *

It was a Saturday, June 21, 1996, five days before my birthday. I went to Creations Beauty Salon, on twentieth street. Mrs. Dorothy Sanders had just put me some "fye" finger rolls in. She had slicked me a nice bang across my forehead and put me under the dryer. I felt a cramp. I was like damn I hope my cycle is not about to come on. It's my birthday weekend. So, I continued to sit there, then I felt something rush out of me that didn't feel normal. I got up and I felt wet, I mean soaked. I looked down at my seat and it was full of blood. I was like "wtf" "My cycle doesn't come on until, after my birthday. I had a towel around my neck, and I had jeans on so you really couldn't see I had messed up my pants so badly. So, I took the towel from around my neck and covered my butt much as I could. I walked up to Mrs. Dot (that was the nickname I called her) I said, "my hair not dry, but I'll let it dry at home. My cycle came on. She said "OK." I paid her and left.

I went home, took my clothes off, got in the shower, and a huge mass of what seemed like a blood clot came out of me. I started screaming. It didn't hurt, it just scared me. I called my mom, and told her what happened, she said "Dee please go to the emergency room now, something isn't right. I put some clothes on and a pad. I got to the emergency room, and they finally called me to the back. The nurse asked when my last cycle was, and the other usual stuff. I said, "my cycle on now for some reason and it's heavy."

I've always dealt with heavy cycles, so it was a thing for me but, this time it was unusual. They had me pee in a cup and ran tests. Later the doctor came in and checked me. To my surprise I had a miscarriage! I was in total disbelief. Like how did this happen? When did this happen? They kept me in the hospital that night and did what they called a DNC. It was uncomfortable, and I was alone.

I didn't tell Shawn at first. Booty was only one almost two. I was on the depo shot, but I guess that shot couldn't handle what Shawn was putting down lol. I wasn't ready for another baby, nor was I ready to add on to my list of responsibilities. I told my mom, what had happened she said, "Dee I knew what was going on, I'm a mother, and a mother knows everything." I called and told Shawn; he was nonchalant about it like its whatever. I often wonder was my baby a boy or girl, or what would I have named him or her. But I looked at it as I dodged a bullet that I couldn't handle. GODS PLAN!!

* * *

It was November, basketball season at Columbus High. Columbus High had just won their game. My girls and I grabbed a pizza and went home. Me and Shawn were on bad terms. I had found out some things. So, we didn't talk. He was at the game and saw me talking to this guy and thought that something was going on. He came over to my house and he had his friend Kito in the car with him. I wouldn't let him in, so then he went back to the car, got a crowbar, and started beating on my door. My neighbors called the police. They weren't aware that I had called my sister Monique. She pulled up around the same time as the police. I looked out the window and Monique was out there. This girl was all up in Shawn face, like she was going to whip him screaming, hit me, hit me you bad. Man, I was killing myself laughing saying, girl if he hit you, you will disappear into thin air lol. The police had Kita and Shawn get out the car, they smelled weed, and arrested them both. He then asked if I wanted to press charges I said "NO!"

The next day I went to visit him and told him it wasn't me that called the police. He said he knew. I felt bad about all of it. I was like I should have just let him in, this wouldn't have happened. Kita was innocent and was only riding in the car with him, and he ended up getting arrested too.

* * *

The drag strip was the hype back then, it was where they would race cars. It was another hot spot-on Sundays. That was me and Monika's hot spot lol. It was like only $5 to get in. We all loved it out there. Guys would race their cars and motorcycles. They had bets on the races and the side bets on who would win. The ladies would only go to see everyone. They didn't have their ass on the races at all. We would get all dolled up just to walk up and down the field just to be seen. We would have our cups of liquor or wine coolers. Some people would bring a portable grill and would grill and sometimes sell food. The races would go on all into the night, race after race.

Then another track we heard about starting to jump. It was in Aberdeen, Mississippi. It was like $10 to get in, some people would hide in the trunk until they got through the gate, so they didn't have to pay. $10 was hard to come by back then lol. It would be like two or three of them in the trunk. I had a Ford Explorer; I could hide like three or four in my trunk. They would cover up and when I pulled through the gate they got out. They eventually caught on to what we were doing and started searching the trunks. It still didn't stop us. We would then leave there and go to West Point Mississippi to club Cimarron. That was our stomping ground after the track on Sundays. Boy the times we used to have in there. We all had ended up dealing with a guy from over there, it was our new stomping ground. They had given us a name "The Hot girls" I really didn't consider myself one lol, my sister Narquita was. Anyway, the song "I Need A Hot Girl" by the Hot Boys was OUR song. People used to clear the floor for us! Soon as we heard the beat, we knew it was our time to show up and show out!

You need a hot one I got one

Deneatrice Ledbetter

I take and bend
Shake it down
Break it down
With me and a friend
Biggity bout slide ride
Work that cat to the right
Push it down
Push it up
Boom you dynamite
Lick it up like ice cream
Nigga you know
To make me bow bow bow bow (Rocky Balboa)
See I lovin it when you thuggin
Baby just don't stop
You could wobledee wobledee (drop drop it like it's hot)
Beat it up and eat it up
Love that's yo dick
And if you ain't from the ghetto
Then ride out bitch
Arms, legs, backs, and breast
You better leave a fucking tax
Nigga manny fresh
Suck it up and yuck it up
Baby work on that hol
Got them niggaz in a circle hollerin here we go o
Back that azz up hea all the way to the zipper
I really love you hot girl but I got to flip her
    I need a hot girl
(What you want boy?)
I want a hot girl
(What you need boy?)
I need a hot girl
(What you want boy?)
I want a hot girl
    I need the highest pricing ho
I can shop with it
Give my ho 10 g's
Tell her to spend the shit
See my hotgirl ride lexus coup , bitch
And she got the matchin roly-o
Floss your shit
And ya got to imagine me for wimp to biff
I see a real hot girl can't defade the disc
Roll the dice
Hit the sev
No crap
No bitch

48

Surv2ved

Got the brand new rover off the shelf real quick
Ruffin my tv's all through that shit
Yokahama 20-inch dubs on that disc
See my cashmoney hot-girl floss her shit
Ridin uptown bumpin hot boys ya bitch
And that blue faced rolex I bought that bitch
Keep big head benjamins on through her shit
Fuck a thug girl
Them hos can cum & suck my dick
I need a hot-girl to represent this uptown shit
    X2
(What you need boy?)
I need a hot girl
(What you want boy?)
I want a hot girl
(What you need boy?)
I need a hot girl
(What you want boy?)
I want a hot girl
    Where my bitch at? look
A hot girl is a silent ho
If a bitch get outta line she a violent ho
Ain't no pest
Far from being a whining ho
Fuck up
She confess, she ain't no lyin ho
That's what I need
A hotgirl is a jazzy bitch
I'd take her any day for a classy bitch
On the downlow for her nigga
She a nasty bitch
I tell her touch it
She gonna try and grab the dick
I bust a nut
It's soft, she get it back hard
The police kick in the door she take the charge
If a nigga goto jail she run for a nigga
Money orders, business ,and go run for a nigga
She be a nigga ballin, would get bout it for her nigga
Lemme come thorugh, hit the stash, and walk up by the nigga
I can't see no other bitch for the B.G.
But a hot girl fo sho call her a H.G. (a hot girl)
    X2
(What you need boy?)
I need a hot girl
(What you want boy?)
I want a hot girl

(What you need boy?)
I need a hot girl
(What you want boy?)
I want a hot girl
    I like'em hot
The onez that don't tell me to stop
Eat dick swallow the cum
And they know how to pop
I need a project bitch, a hoodrat bitch
One that don't give a fuck and say she took that bitch
    She a doggy wit it
She gon wobbledee
Then she know I'm da want it wit it
Open her legs and squeeze a nigga
Like she want me in it
Now turn around and back it up
Then throw it at a nigga
Tell her I say"ohh that's enuff"
    Give me a gansta ho
One that don't give a fuck
And thata shank the ho
The one that'll slang still
And keep it on the low
One that'll do time for me
And slang that fuckin co
To all you know
    A little shorty gettin and try to have ya hurtin and thumpin
They be like he small girl he workin with something
Lil' Wayne on fire I'll smash on your boo before a hot girl bang
What's the matter with you?
    X2
(What you need boy?)
I need a hot girl
(What you want boy?)
I want a hot girl
(What you need boy?)
I need a hot girl
(What you want boy?)
I want a hot girl
    Understand look,
That's a motherfuckin hot boy$
Definition of a motherfuckin hotgirl
Do you see what I'm saying?
It's all gravy
If you fit the description
Then come on get with a nigga
Come on get with a nigga

If you think its ???
Come get wit a nigga

The girls would have the big bamboo earrings, Duck Head™, Guess™, Tommy Hilfiger™, Ivy Crew™. Levis™, Jordache™ jeans, LA Gear™, Rebooks™, British Knights™, Roca Wear™, Allstars™, Addidas™, and Dexter™ shoes. We loved our red lipstick! The older people use to say wearing red lipstick was for Hoes, and Tramps. We didn't care, we still wore sneakers to match. We used to go to Creations Beauty Salon, to get the French roll, and banana peels. Sometimes even finger waves, with a hint of color. We had so much gel and sprits on our hair that the strongest storm could come through and our hair still wouldn't move. We used to paint our own nails and toes back then. We would go to the ten-cent store and buy mood lipstick. It would have our lips so shiny you could fry a whole pot of chicken. We had clock purses, or the purses we hand made from the cool aid pouches, and good eyeliner, which was all we needed to complete our look. Our parents would drop us off at the mall, with our friends, we would walk the mall for hours, just hanging out. Going to the arcade room to play games, etc. We had a certain time that we had to be out in front of the mall, so our parents could pick us up. If you weren't at that door at a certain time, your ass wasn't going back anymore.

The store Reeds was my favorite store. Even though I couldn't afford anything in there I would go in to try on some of the clothes in the dressing room, and look in the mirror and, say I'll be able to afford these one day. The movie theatre was in the mall also. You could go into the back entrance, and it sat to your right. It was small, but to us back then it was big. We would all plan at school to meet up to go see a movie. We really weren't in there watching it. It was a way to get out of the house on the weekends sometimes. Radio Shack was where we mostly got our electronics. Then we had Prestige Clothing, and Sam's was everyone guy. He had the latest urban wear for the girls and guys. Baby Phat™, Apple Bottoms™, Beyounce™, LRG™, just to name a few. Sam had my number and would call me when he had new arrivals.

I've always had a bad shopping problem, I mean always. I would buy so many clothes and shoes, and never wore even half. I was getting stuff just to say I had it. There was a jewelry store that was called "Accessory Connor" that's where most people got their jewelry from. They also sold purses and other things. The guy that owned it was super cool, and his daughter went to school with me for a little while. Everyone in town basically liked him because he was down to earth. He fixed all his merchandise if something was wrong. He would fix it or replace it. He also did jewelry repair, and ear piercing.

Deneatrice Ledbetter

Chapter 5 *The Power of Tongues!*

At age twenty-one I got married to who I thought at the time was the love of my life. He wanted a child, a girl since he already had a boy. I ended up pregnant and it was a boy, what I really wanted. I had his name already made up, it was supposed to have been Jaylen, but his dad wanted a junior. He had a son already named Chris, but not Chris junior. So, I set aside what I wanted to give my son the name his father wanted him to have. So, we named him Christopher LaShawn Harris Jr., We called him pooh as a child, because he put me in the mind of Winnie the Pooh. He was a big crybaby for one, and so spoiled. My cousin Lisha basically kept him until he was about three. She took care of him like he was her own, her and Charles did. She was always there for him even now that he is grown, she still calls him Pooh. As he got older, he would get mad when we called him pooh in public. Chris was my only son and last baby. I had him so spoiled that it messed me up. He got anything he could ever ask for as a child. I remember once he came home from school and told me "Mom the kids at school said we are rich" I was like why would they say that? He said, "because I wear new clothes and have on different shoes every day." I said baby "we are far from rich, we are comfortable." This has spoiled him into adulthood because he stills to this day thinks he can have whatever he wants. He is a hard-working young man, proud is an understatement.

The marriage life was hard. Marriage isn't something that can be taught. You must learn as you go. You never really know a person until you either live together or you get married. Boy, did I learn a lesson. My husband was a great provider; he was handsome; he took care of the home and made sure the kids were good. But other women were his weakness. With him being well known, and a big dealer, that made him even more popular. I could deal with that, but the only downfall was that he was in and out of jail.

Back in the day girls loved a man that had the flashy cars, gold teeth, gold chains, rings, earrings, and a pocket full of money. Let's not leave out cars with big rims, and loud music. The music would be so loud you could feel it through your chest. Some of the guys even had chandeliers in their cars, those were the days. Dealing with him in and out of jail put a dark cloud over our marriage. He felt as if he was still taking care of home from the jail cell, he was doing what he needed to do financially. I had the money to take care of the home and the children, but no emotional, physical, help. Raising three children alone. Making sure that had shelter, food, and their needs were met. Homework, school functions, baseball, and basketball games. Their first heartbreaks, emotional state, the list goes on and on. What I needed the most was him there.

Marriage takes two people. Not one with money, and the other handling everything else. It messes with your mental state. Having a two-parent household, by two people who trying, helps with your children, in many ways. 50/50 is something I've always believed in, in all areas in a marriage and household. Yes, a man supposes to be the head, but that's to lead his family, not take all the responsible of taking care of home all by himself. Yet, let him be the head of what is best for his family. While the mother takes care of the household needs, and children. Work as a team, never just delegate a task to just one person, do it together and teach each other. Make moves together and overcome obstacles that are thrown to get you off track.

Nineteen ninety-nine was the year that our world crashed before our eyes April 24, 1999, the last year of the nineteenth century. People often said the world end that year, and we wouldn't make it to the 2000's. Little did I know my sister Monique wouldn't make it. I always felt it should have been me. Because I was the bad child, I was the one hard-headed. I was the one that was hot headed, and disobedient. Why I deserved to live, why I deserve to be here. Monique was the perfect child to me, she was outgoing, obedient, respectful, an overachiever, a role model. But instead, she was taken. I felt for years she didn't deserve that, I questioned GOD why he didn't take me instead. Why did I get to stay with my children, and she couldn't. I felt she deserved to be here more than me.

My mom was my strength. She watched her daughter get killed in her own yard, her mother gets killed sitting right next to her. And a husband that was on drugs and was verbally abusive. All the strength I have I gained from her. Strong is not a strong enough word to describe her.

My sister death left so many rumors, unanswered questions, lies, hurt and pain. The person that shot that 9-millimeter gun that night, is thinking in the back of their heads to this day, was it me, that shot and killed an innocent bystander that night. Took her from her babies to leave for her mother to raise. Shan'Qula and Tierra did not deserve this senseless act to happen to their mother. Qula was only three years old, and Tiera was ten days old. How fair is that to a child? How do you explain to them that their mother was taken before they really got a chance to get to know their mother.

Gun violence is something that will be around until the end of time. We as a community need to come together because we lose loved ones every minute of every day. Life is supposed to be lived upon GOD calling, not man. We must live everyday like it is our last. One day you can be on top of the world, and the next day the world will be on top of you. People these days are snapping out in the blink of an eye. Ask yourself would you be able to handle ALL of this and still function daily like nothing was wrong.

I always felt she was my mother's favorite child. My mothers face would glow from even the mention of

Monique name. Reflecting on that night, the hurt, and pain, on my mother's face is a picture I'll never forget. It was like my mother gave up after Monique death. She lost weight, found out she was a diabetic, had high blood pressure, and found out she had congested heart failure. It was like she had given up on life at one point. She once told me that, she wanted to live to see Monique children to be grown and able to take care of their selves. I never questioned why she said that until later in life it all made sense. My mom evidently stopped working, and started getting her disability, because her health would no longer let her stay working at Sandersons Plumbing. It took a while for them to approve her because the process was so long. My grandmother, who was her mother, we called her mom, helped my mother the entire time until she was approved.

My grandmother would come to my mother's house and cook, clean, go with her to doctors' appointments, and help with anything else she needed. She helped everyone that needed her in our family. She was a true soldier, I always wondered where my mother got her strength from, it was defiantly from her. My mother was a resilient woman, a once and a lifetime mother, sister, wife, and friend. They don't make them like her anymore.

Losing a sister is a different feeling. You grow up with them, sleep in the same bed as them, do basically everything with them. I reflect on the night she was laying lifeless on the ground. Her eyes were wide open looking at me so, I thought. Her chest was getting so big, it's strange that I could see that in the midnight light. Just to find out later she was bleeding on the inside. That drove me absolutely crazy for years. I held a lot inside because I didn't want anyone to feel pity for me. I think back often on what I could have done differently. What could I have done to save my sister. I even blamed myself for years thinking, I helped killed her. Because I was giving her chest compression and just pushing the bullet in further. I felt so empty, alone, afraid, and clueless.

I went into the kitchen the next day after the shooting. My mom was sitting at the kitchen table alone. It was in the early hours of the morning. She had her hands folded praying to GOD asking, "why my baby LORD, why, my baby"? She didn't deserve to die"! To see my mother like that tore me apart. I'm an overthinker I always have been.

I started to think, does she wish it was me instead, would that make her feel better"? As, I walked into the kitchen, she never stopped begging, crying, and asking GOD why. I went over to her and asked, "mom is you ok" she scolded me and yes "leave me alone, Dee, just leave me alone." I felt worthless, and mad. I didn't know how she felt, but I know how I felt, and that was like shit. No number of words could make any one of us feel better.

Death is something that we all will encounter one day, you cannot run from it, and you can't hide, when it's your time it's your time. People would come over all day every day for a week. Giving cards, money, flowers, food, drinks, water, you name it. My aunt Linda my father's sister was GOD sent. She came and helped, cleaned, and she kept the kids until things calmed down. She would bring them over daily to see Mother. The day came for the wake and all the family and friends gathered. It was so hard seeing my sister's body lying there. She had a beautiful smile on her face. She looked at peace. There wasn't even a sign that she wasn't living if it wasn't for the funeral home. She had braids in her hair, they had a little color in them, it was braided into a bob style. She had on a black pants suit with a red shirt underneath. They had some make-up on her but not a lot, with some soft color lipstick. I bent down and kissed her forehead. I wasn't even scared; I remember as a small child I feared dead people from watching all the movies and stuff. But, to me she looked like she was sleeping.

People started taking out cameras, taking pictures of her. My mom got furious. I never understood why people took pictures of their love's ones in a casket. That's not something I want to relive by seeing the pictures of someone laying in a casket. After the wake, we gathered back at my mother's house. Her house was full of people. My mother wasn't up for all the company because she was exhausted, and overwhelmed. People were still bringing food, drinks, cards, and letting us know that we were in their prayers. The day finally came for the funeral, we had the time scheduled later than usual. I think it was at four o'clock in the afternoon. That was because we had to wait on Pastor Boyd to get in. The limos came to the house and got us and took us around the corner to our church Zion Gate Missionary Baptist Church. We pulled up to the church and we sat in the Limo watching people walk into the church to give their respects to my dear sister Moinque, one last time. As we got out of the limo, they started lining us up. They put mother and father beside each other, and my mother immediately grabbed me and my sister's hands. She did not want him to touch her, due to what he did when we were putting the obituary together.

My dad went and got my brothers so they could walk in with us, this made my mom even more pissed. My father felt as if he could do as he pleased no matter who felt the hurt, or the consequences. It seemed like whatever he said went. At the funeral Pastor Boyd asked who had any kind words to say. Her friend Ebony stood up; Ebony was friends with all of us. She spoke a few words, and it broke me down. A few others got up to speak. I looked over at my mother and she had a look on her face of disappointment, pain, and frustration all at the same time. It was like she was lost. Seeing my mother like that made me angry. A child never wants to see their mother hurt. That's a different kind of hurt. We left the church and went to the grave site. The grave site was just as packed as the funeral. We gathered there and said our last goodbyes.

Chris had a side business, cleaning cars, it was basically

a detail shop. That was one of his cover ups. He had a great clientele. Saturdays were his biggest days. He would help his workers detail the cars. He has never been a lazy person and would always work. One day my son went with him to help clean cars on a Saturday morning. Keep in mind he was only around three or four at the time. They were there and were cleaning cars basically all that day. When my son got home, he had a pocket full of change. I asked him where you get all that change from,

He said, "my daddy girlfriend."

I laughed and said, "whatever boy."

He said, "I promise my daddy girlfriend did give me that change."

His dad then said, "Boy shut up my cousin gave you that money."

At that moment I knew something was up. I waited until Chris left and I started questioning him again. I knew that wasn't the right thing to do because children will tell the truth when it's being told to someone else and hurt your feelings while telling it. So, I asked him who was his dad's girlfriend that gave him that money. He told me her name. It was the girl that I was hearing about around town that he was messing with. The crazy part is his own mother told me also. Lil Chris said, "we got her car and cleaned it, me and my daddy, and she has a lot of change in her car door, and I asked her could I have it and she said yes, and I got all of it."

I then asked, "what else did you all do?"

He said, "she took me to McDonalds in her car and got me a happy meal with a toy. Then she took me back with my daddy, and she kissed him. And I said, "Nastttyyy!"

At this point my blood was boiling, I wasn't mad about the kiss, because I hate kissing, I was pissed because they did it in front of my son. Then he goes to tell me, "She told me she's, my stepmom." I lost it at that very moment. I found her number. It wasn't hard at all. I cussed the bitch out from A-Z. For one you didn't birth my child, and for two the man you are sleeping with is married. She sat there in silence, and didn't say a word, and hung up once she got tired of hearing me screaming at her through the phone. I guess. Like, how can you be out in the streets sexing someone else husband, but scary. Not knowing I'm a whole fool and don't play, win, lose or draw. I saw my mother put up with it and I be dammed if I did. My phone rang, it was my husband asking me why I called that girl going off like that. I told him what my son told me, that was a big mistake. I told him to bring his ass home and we would talk. He took too long so I went and found his ass, at the car wash. I acted a damn fool in front of all his homies, he just looked at me and, called me crazy.

When he got home later, I let his ass have it. My mouth is big, my voice is loud, and I Deneatrice WILL always get the last word in an argument. I lit his ass up. I went all the way in, I even hit below the belt. He told my son that he shouldn't have told me that lie. Why confuse a child in between a lie and the truth? Why even put them in a position to pick what to say, when the truth is the truth? Or even pick between his parents on who side to be on. My son started crying, and I consoled him, Chris got mad, and said he's a boy, I said yes, he is but he's my child and I will protect him. I don't give a damn what society says about showing young boys compassion when their feelings are hurt. They are still human. After that incident, me and my son have been clicked tight since, a true mother's son.

I woke up one morning around three-thirty. I was tossing and turning in my bed, and it was storming outside.

I had on some shorts and a tank top. I got up, went outside to my car, opened my glove compartment, pulled out a gun and put it to my head. I spoke these words, "I'm just tired." I said it repeatedly. I got out of the car in the rain, and tears overflowing, asking, and pleading with GOD. WHY? I know you were never supposed to question HIM, but I just couldn't understand why all this was happening. My neighbor came out screaming, "DON'T DO IT!" and grabbed and held me and rocked me like a baby. She just kept rocking me, holding me, and talking to God in tongues. She held me like a newborn baby, as she screamed, (DEMON RELEASE HER IN THE NAME OF JESUS, BIND ALL EVIL SPIRITS, TAKE YOUR HAND OFF HER RIGHT NOW, I REBUKE ALL SADNESS AND HURT, AND PAIN, RIGHT NOW IN THE MIGHTY NAME OF JESUS.

I never told a soul about that night. A total stranger that I really didn't know, who I thought was a nosey neighbor, help saved me that night. At that point I started to be mindful of how I speak or talk to people. You never know what they are going through or what's on their mind at that very moment, which could make them want to end it all by just a trigger word. One trigger word could drive a person to end it all. I was fighting secrets battles, hidden demons, hurt, pain, and embarrassment daily. Just remember that one day this could be YOU. Be slow to JUDGE, and quick to PRAY.

Deneatrice Ledbetter

Chapter 6 *From Mother to Grandmother!*

We had just got a big house in Roanoke Circle, in Columbus Ms. Four bedrooms, with two baths, double carport, with a bug back yard. He didn't want to move to Columbus, but we did anyway. One morning he woke me out of my sleep screaming. We had a fireplace, and a possum came through it. My husband was screaming and running through the house scared. We all were scared it was like six o'clock in the morning and the kids were getting ready to catch the bus for school. I ran out of the house onto the street. Chris, my husband, went around the corner and got his cousin Ronnie, to help get it out of the house. Me and Ronnie's wife Stephanie, we clicked tight. She has two daughters, Rhonda and Qula. They were like family even until this day. She came around there with him. Me and her were laughing so hard at them they both were scared. They used the excuse that they didn't want to get close to it because it would scratch their eyes out. They ended up not finding the possum nowhere.

Finally, they looked around and it was on the table

looking at them and we all took off again. They finally started beating on it with the broom and got it out of the house. That was the funniest shit ever. I went to work. I had daycare at that time and the kids went to school. Chris called me around lunch time and told me that the possum had come back through the chimney again. I told him I wasn't coming home until it was out of there. By the time we got home that evening the possum was gone. It took weeks for us to get back on track, because every time we went into the living room we thought about that possum.

I had hit at the casino for $ 18,000 and some change and got myself an F-150. I wanted that truck so bad, I've always loved music, so I took it to Hooper in Columbus Mississippi, and had two 12'S put in it. It hit so hard; it made your chest thump lol. The kids loved me dropping them off at school and wanted me to turn the music up loud when I dropped them off. Especially my son Chris. Time went by, things were going well, the daycare was going great, all the kids' needs were met, eating good, all the latest cars, clothes, shoes, you name it. Then it happened again! I was lying in bed when I got a call and the voice on the other end of the phone said, "Dee, they got him" I already knew what they were talking about. Anyway, that was the vehicle my husband was driving when they pulled him over. They found drugs on him and took him to jail. I was devastated, for one he was locked up again, and for two my truck was impounded. They arranged it for him, the next morning. He always had top notched lawyers. They were able to get my truck, released so I went to the tow yard and picked my baby up. They evidently gave my husband a bond, he came home, but only for a little while before he was sentenced. They gave him eight years, none suspended due to being a third time offender. This was ok when he first left because he left us in good shape. We had good money in the bank and the daycare was still doing good.

It was the Friday after Thanksgiving, and it was my mom's tradition to go Black Friday shopping every single year after Thanksgiving. It was me, my mom, and my sister Narquita. They had brought Qula, Olivia, Jeremy, Tierra, and Cameron to stay with my kids while we were out shopping. We were in Walmart when I got a call saying, "Mom Dashea fell through the attic, and burst her chin." I panicked. We dropped everything and went straight to my house. When we pulled up to the house, under the carport the entire ceiling was gone. We walked into the house and my baby chin was wide open. Tears were in my eyes because it looked like she was in so much pain.

Come to find out my bad ass son, nieces, and nephews, crawled their ass up in the attic playing and, Dashea, and Qula went up there and tried to fix it before we got home, and fell through into the garage. That's how her chin burst wide open. I took her to the emergency room. When we got there, they gave her something for pain, and cleaned the wound. Instead of stiches they had a new method where they glued it back together. I was super pissed; my baby chin was messed up and she was trying to keep her cousins from getting in trouble. Secondly it was over eight hundred dollars to fix the ceiling over my garage. On top of that it was close to Christmas, and I wasn't even halfway done with Christmas shopping. After that day I told my mom nobody's kids can come back to my house when I'm not there. Qula was the Only one that could come. She and Dashea were like blood sisters, and she wasn't bad like the others lol. I had to pay for the repairs myself. But when I got it fixed it looked brand new like it hadn't ever been damaged.

I had a birthday party after I got back from Jamaica, I really needed some fun after all the stress I was under from the unforeseen circumstances. This is when my depression started kicking in, full force. You ever heard the quote "I'm fading away, and no one is noticing. That was me. All, because I hid it well. I would smile when things got tough, I would party, drink, dance to cover my sadness. I would make others happy when I felt so empty inside. I felt like I had to be strong for the public eye. I was thirty years old, married with three children, A daycare owner, nice house, and cars, but in the inside I was miserable. I was putting up with things that I shouldn't have put up with. I was handling everyone's problems but mine.

As a child I basically raised my sisters at a young age. I couldn't participate in school activities much because my mom worked 3-11 at Sanderson Plumbing, and my dad was on drugs and was in the streets. So, I was the one that had to make sure homework was done, and that they ate supper every night. So, I never got to experience how to be a child, from the age of nine until like fifteen. I was doing adult duties. I could cut a whole chicken up and fry it by the age of twelve. I had to wash dishes, clean, make sure they had their clothes out, and iron for the next school day.

As I reflect on those years, I felt I lost time. I couldn't do what my age group was doing because I had to grow up fast. Even Tho my dad wasn't there, he was so strict that we had to be in the house before the streetlight turned on. And the killing part was we were only on the porch. We couldn't leave the yard. IF we let that streetlight catch us outside of that door an ass whopping, I got. I was accountable for everything. It was always my fault even if my sisters did it. I do not remember once my father whipping my sisters, not once. I felt like I was his punching bag. Even when he was mad at others, I caught all his anger. Back when I got rapped, he wasn't there for me, he honestly thought I was lying, until years later. That scared me for life.

The rape took place on a Saturday evening. We were alone, while he was rapping me, he never said a word. I was trying to push him off me. But he overpowered me. It didn't last long. And he did not even use a condom. He pulled out when he got ready to ejaculate. In his and his wife's own bed, how sick is that? For years I could still feel and smell his breath on my neck. I would be in disgust. His jerry curl activator he used on his hair I could smell it. It wore his hair in some weird way, I can't even explain. When he left when he got finished, he never even said a word, not even for me not to tell, like he knew I wouldn't, or no one would believe me. He was so cocky. Everyone seemed afraid of him, he really didn't talk much when he was around our family. He was always weird to me.

After, I came out of the bathroom when he left, I went into their closet and he had a gun, between the blankets. I found it because for one I'm nosey, and for two I use to clean the house from top to bottom. I pulled the gun out, went into the bathroom, and put it to my head. I felt this was all my fault, and that no one would believe me anyway. I didn't really know how to pray, but I knew GOD, who was enough to save me from, losing myself for eternity. Plus, I feared him, and it seemed as if my family was also. I sat on the floor by the toilet and cried, wanting to end my life as a teenager for something that a man, who was my uncle that I looked up to, and was supposed to protect me, rapped me instead. He walked around and came around my family like he didn't do anything to me. I would catch him looking at my sister and some of my other cousins, but I watched him like a hawk, he wasn't about to attack anyone else if I could prevent it.

We were all down at my grandmother's house in Brooksville Mississippi, one third Sunday. Third, Sunday was when we would all gather at my grandmother's house and go to church, and eat a big feast after church, all my mom's brothers and sisters that lived in the area would come down and fellowship together. All my cousins were there so we could catch up. My grandmother would cook mostly all the food, but we couldn't eat until my mom got there to fry the chicken. No one could cook chicken like her. My mom and aunts use to love when it was basketball season, they were Jordan fans, because my aunt Lilly, and uncle Randy lived in Chicago at the time. When he was playing, they loved the way he licked his tongue when he was about to dunk the ball once. They melted in their chairs. We started laughing (the children, myself, and cousins). They made us get out and told us to go play.

One thing my grandparents, parents, aunts, uncles, any grownups for that matter did not play about children sitting in grown people faces. We couldn't even use the word lie to this day it's a cuss word to the older generation.

We were packing up to go plates to go back home to Columbus, which was like a thirty-minute drive. My aunt Mary and her children had to ride back to Columbus with us this Sunday. So, it wasn't enough room in our car for everyone. My aunt said I could ride back home with her. I immediately said no, my mom knew why, and for some reason I believe my grandmother knew why. It was the way she looked at me when I said it, then she looked over at my mom. My mom then said to one of my little cousins, you ride with them. I think that's the first time I said no, to a grown -up. The crazy part was no one didn't punish me for saying it, nor did I get in trouble. When I think back on that incident, I wonder why no one ever said a word. Did they know? Or was it just overlooked because of who he was?

Life just kept on going, I went out of the country for the first time, and it was to Montego Jamicia. It was for my birthday. It was my 26th birthday, since then I've been 26 ever since lol. I had a birthday party planned before I left and went. The incident that happened at the airport made me want to cancel, from embarrassment, humiliation, and I was exhausted. But then I remembered who I was and got myself together and said the show must go on. Things started to get back on track, daycare was still running smoothly, the kids doing great, life was taking a turn for the better. I met this guy that I had known forever. He used to always try to talk to me, but he wasn't my type at all, well so I thought. He was funny, he kept me laughing, and another thing, that man loved me like a man was supposed to love a woman, he catered to me even when I was mad at him, or if he was mad at me. People use to tell me all the time "Dee, he beat women," but for the first two years he never laid one had on me, even at times when I made him mad enough to do so. Even the incident when he shot himself, he wasn't violent that night. He used to drink Tanqueray, who was some strong ass Gin, I think the strongest on the market. He would drink an entire bottle when he would drink it. If it wasn't for drinking that night would never have happened, but it did and it made me realize that life can flash before your eyes in a few seconds. I could have been dead and gone, leaving my children, for my mother to raise, because she had already lost one child to gun violence. It taught me to live one day at a time and live it like it's my last. It made me make better decisions in life and made be because a different woman.

Violence is never ok, not any point, or for any reason. If you see any signs, get out, don't stay for love, or convenience, it could cost you your life. If you must start completely over, do it GOD got you. It's better to be at peace than living in fear, especially from someone you love. Abuse can happen physically, and verbally it will have you doubting your self-worth, or mental. It will make you feel worthless, and make you feel as if you aren't wanted. Learn to love self-first because if you don't, how can you love anyone else? You must be stronger than your thought. And always remember you must HEAL, to be HEAL.

We were out at a party at the Elks Lodge one night, me and my cousin Doug. People thought we used to date because we were always together. His mom and my mom are sisters. Anyway, we were together the whole night.

After the club closed, we went to the Huddle House, that's where everyone would go after the club, that's the night when I found out my boyfriend was violent. After this incident, I decided that we should go our separate ways. Because it was affecting me mentally, and my children. They would look so sad when things got bad. I never wanted them to see any of that, because it influences children, and I didn't want them to grow up making the same mistakes I did. I had my babies young, I was wild and, in the streets, because I never got to enjoy my childhood due to me having to grow up too fast as the older people say. So, my mom would watch my children because I partied, drank, hung out, or whatever I did. I often wondered did my mom helped me with the kids because of what I had to go through as a child, when I was a young adult in a child's body.

Once, my dad was beating me for something I had done, and she came into the room and told him that's enough. He continued to beat me, and I remembered I looked at him and said, "Daddy I can't take no more." He looked at me with rage in his eyes and hit me a few more times and stopped. He told me that night if I ever say that to him again, he will beat me worse. When I walked out of the room my mom had a sad look on her face. My sisters were sitting on the bed with a sad look on their face, they always felt sorry for me. My mom had this sad look on her face, like she wanted to comfort me, but she couldn't. Most of the time she was at work, but some of the times she was there. She wasn't scared of him; I just don't know why she didn't stop. That's a question I used to want to ask my mom, but never built the courage to ask her. I guess that's why I took the abuse like I did, because I was so used to getting beaten as a child.

My mom wasn't an affectionate person, but we knew she loved us with everything in her. My dad loved us also, the drugs just cloud his judgment. Since my parents didn't show love out loud, I made sure I told my children love them, I'm proud of them, and I'm always there for them. I wanted and needed to be different from how I was raised up. I wanted to be better, as a mother, and a parent. I didn't always get it right when it came to my kids, I made many mistakes, but they can always say my mom loved us, and would put the world on her shoulders for us.

My children were very athletic, unlike me. They got it

from my dad, all I got was my dad's blood, and demeanor, and some of his ways. But the athletic part missed me lol. My oldest Ta'Dashea was good at softball, she was the pitcher and second baseman. She also was one of the best cheerleaders around, she received a scholarship from Scooba Tech, for cheerleading. So, she cheered in high school and college. Ka'Daryal was awesome in softball, fastpitch, and Basketball. My son Chrsitopher was good at Baseball and being the class clown. I also had nieces and nephews that played as well. They all were good. My mom didn't miss a game even if she was sick. She still managed to get herself together and make sure her presence was there. My mom really loved basketball season at Columbus High. We had assigned seats at the top of the bleachers when you first walked in the gym. We had our own section. It used to be me, my mom, Jordynn my grandbaby, my sister Narquita, Stephanie, Rhonda, Qula, Tiny, and the twins. My mom had players she liked to watch on the boys' team, since none of our boys played basketball there. She would be fussing and cussing when they messed up you would have thought she was one of their mothers.

When Booty would play, she would brag so much about Booty to people in the crowd. That woman was all her children, and grandchildren biggest supporter. She would sneak in snacks in her purse because she said the concession stand was just too high. No matter where we went my mother had her snacks, sandwiches, and drinks but she didn't play lol. She even traveled with them to off games, especially softball season. The children played ball in Prost Park every summer, we would travel to different cities to watch our babies play ball. Qula, who is my sister child Monique, was awesome when it came to hitting a softball. We would make of cheers, clap, stomped, and would have a good ole time. Our children were looking to make sure we were there, if we even mumbled we couldn't make a game that would mess up their day.

Booty my youngest daughter "she got that nickname as a child from her dad" was in the eighth grade and the coach at the time felt as if Booty was good enough to play on varsity, even though she had Seniors, sitting on the beach that wanted to play. Anyway, we were at a game in Maben, Mississippi. It was a Saturday. The coach put my daughter in to run for someone because they weren't good runners. When she ran to third base she turned to go home, the coach was trying to tell her to run to the bag but didn't turn because they could get her out. She was running at fast paste, and couldn't stop, and she ended up getting out trying to dive back on base. At this point, the coach started fussing and cussing her out, Booty then started to cry that sent me in defense mode. She then screamed out to my child right in my face and said you fucking tidy baby. That's when I lost it. I called her everything but, the child of GOD. The game ended and we were walking back to our cars, and the children getting back on the bus to go home. I was on the phone with my husband at the time, telling him what was going on. The coach then, approached me and I had my hand in her face, and I pushed her in the face and told her I don't play about my children, and you approach the right bitch on the wrong day. She then goes to say my children couldn't get back on her bus to go home. I asked her "are you serious" she said 'yes, your children can't get back on my bus, you take them home!' Thankfully, I had driven my daycare van to the game because they would not have a way home.

The next day I get a call saying I'm suspended from all the games the rest of the season. I was furious, like what did I do, this woman kicked my children off the bus with no way home or nothing. They were her responsibility, they were in her care, but she took it upon herself to do a vicious act. I then went to the school board to be out on their agenda for the upcoming school board meeting. I sent emails to every single member on the panel, before the meeting which was on that following Tuesday. I received a call letting me know I was granted the chance to get on the agenda. When they finally got to my name on the agenda, I stood up and pleaded my case. My mother, children and a few others were there to support. I told them 'My version" of the story since she had given them hers. It's always three sides to a story theirs, yours, and the truth. I told them I was wrong for pointing my finger in her face, and pushing her, which left a scratch on her nose that I wasn't even aware that I did, until the meeting. I guess when I was pointing in her face my fingernail scratched her nose. I explained to them that they left my children in danger, because she the coach left my children without rides home, while in her care. Anyway, the panel thanked me for my concerns, and told me they will follow up with me about their decision no later than the next day. I got a call first, telling me I could attend all upcoming games, and the coach had been terminated from her duties as coach. "At first they told me I still couldn't come back the rest of the season" then I got a call saying I could. That was not what I wanted, I only wanted an apology, but the school board felt as if she deserted my children while in her care, which she did. The team suffered a little after that, but then they got coach Jammie, and she was awesome, and had passion for the children on the team like they were her own.

On April 28, 2011, my first grand daughter was born. The love I have for her is unexplainable. Dashea name her "Jordynn Kenndy Ward" I asked Dashe once why she gave her two first names, she said she liked both names but, didn't know which one to pick, so she name her both, lol. Jordynn lights up the room no matter where she went. She was the most beautiful, big bright eyed, spoiled, crybaby you have ever met. She was my mom's joy. My niece Tierra used to tell me how spoiled and how she would kick the back of my mom's seat when she was driving when she got mad or couldn't have her way. The way Tierra and Qula would act out how she used to kick my mom's seat in her car was hilarious and funny. I couldn't stop laughing. My mom would get mad at them for telling me, because she didn't want to get in trouble, because I didn't play children being disrespectful. I would ask Jordynn why she did that; she would break down and cry and say, "Nanna they are telling a story on me, I didn't do that"! My grandbabies call me Nanna. I don't play that grandmother shit at all! I became a grandmother at an early age. I was 35 years old. I wanted another child, a boy, to be exact, but after Jordynn came that was a big NO, and plus my children told me I didn't need any more children. So, I got a dog and named him Chase.

Bubba brought me that dog for Valentines Day one year. He acts just like a child, you must feed him, clothe him, find a babysitter when needed, so he was considered my fourth child. Jordynn. Me having another child was out the question anyway because I like to travel, and up and go when I'm ready with no, worries. Jordynn has the athletic side from her mom and dad. Dashea was an awesome softball player and cheerleader. Her dad

Perrance was a great football player. She gets it from both sides. Jordynn played ball in the park, at Post Park. My mom made all her grandchildren play, even if she was the one to pay for it. I think her watching her grandchildren, grow, and playing sports is what helped keep her going daily. Jordynn was good at it, and she enjoyed it.

Every year for Jordynn birthday I would take her to a different state to explore. My parents never really took us anywhere, because for one we couldn't afford it and for two my mom worked so much. I would take Jordynn and my GOD daughter Dyiamond on cruises to the Bahamas, Mexico. To Disney World in Orlando Florida. Anywhere her heart desired. Dyiamond was just like my own, I became her GOD mother when she was around eight or nine. I always knew Dyiamond mom, because she was the daughter of my childhood friend who passed away from cancer. She would come stay with me and my family on holidays, family gatherings, trips, etc. She was a few years older than Jordynn, but they clicked like blood sisters.

My mother had Jordynn basically until she left this world for the most part. My mom would let Jordynn do ANYTHING she wanted, at any time. Spoiled is not a big enough word for Jordynn. Once I was at my mom house washing Jordynn hair. She was extremely tender headed like me, her mother Dashea. We got bad hair, well I do anyway. So, I was washing her hair in my mother kitchen sink, and Jordynn was acting a fool as usual while washing her hair. She had me so upset because she was crying, and the water really hadn't touched her yet. (She only did that when my mother was around). Anyway, my mother walked into the kitchen where we were. And she walked over to the sink and tried to grab Jordynn to let her know its ok, and she was saying to me "Dee don't handle her so rough like that."

For a minute I snapped, I said "move mom, you the reason she like she is now!" I went back down to Bubba's house afterwards, my mind was so heavy, and my peace was disturbed. I got so angry at myself for talking to my mother like that. I went to bed, and I tossed and turned all night long. Because I kept thinking about how I talked to her, and the look on her face of hurt, for me saying those words. It was around 11:00 P.M. I picked up the phone and called my mother and apologized to her. I told her I'm sorry, and I would never scream, or disrespect her again. She replied "ok Dee" I could tell she was tired and was sleeping when I called. The next day I went back over to my mother's house. I told her to her face I was sorry, to be honest It still didn't make me feel any better. For days all I could see was that look on my mother's face, it took me back to the times my dad disappointed her. I made a vow I would never in my life, or her life do that again. We often take our parents for granted, and when they are gone, they are gone, it's no time to get it right because they are no longer here. I'm a firm believer you reap what you sow, that's not only a saying, but it's also the truth. I never understood why some people didn't have a relationship with their mom. Although for dads that a normal these days, but for mother I just don't see how.

Mothers are the ones who make the world go around. They raise us from babies to adulthood, in most cases. They make sure we are fed and sheltered. They comfort us when are sick, stay up long nights rocking or rubbing you to sleep. They are there when their daughters or sons have their first heartbreak. They are there cheering you on in the stands and seeing you off to college. Mothers are the most resilient and nurturing creatures alive today.

Chapter 7 *The End Again*

Mothers are the ones who make the world go around. They raise us from babies to adulthood, in most cases. They make sure we are fed and sheltered. They comfort us when are sick, stay up long nights rocking or rubbing you to sleep. They are there when their daughters or sons have their first heartbreak. They are there cheering you on in the stands and seeing you off to college. Mothers are the most resilient and nurturing creatures alive today.

It was 2014 Life was really "LIFING" at this point. I was working at Mercedes and decided I wanted a change in life. I talked it over with my cousin Monika, and she welcomed me with open arms. She even got me a job at her place of employment. I moved on April 28, 2014, on Jordynn's 3rd birthday. I cried all the way there. It was so late at night. I had left extremely late because I was not sure was I ready for this big move. Once I got there, I settled in, and was about to start my job within a few hours. I was so exhausted the next morning because for one I couldn't get any sleep and for two I was nervous, and anxious. I had set myself a goal to at least give Atlanta a try for six months. Every weekend for the next three months I was on the highway going back to Mississippi. For one, to see my mom. She was in ok health, but I could see that her sickness was weighing her down.

Once she got mad at me and my niece Qula. We were joking about something, and my mom got mad and said "yall are going to mis me when I'm gone!" I would always say to her girl you aren't going nowhere. She had been to the doctor earlier that day, and the doctor gave her some news, she wouldn't tell us, she said she was taking that secret to her grave. At that time, I really didn't listen, and when I say listen, I mean listen how she said it. I always think back to that day and wonder what he told her. One thing I did know was that she was sixty years old but her heartbeat like a ninety-year-old woman. When I found out at first it kind of scared me. She looked ok, and fine to me, so I didn't worry as much at first.

Georgia life was great when school let out Chris came on to live with me. He stayed back in Mississippi to complete his last year in junior high. He would start high school fresh in Georgia. I got him registered for school, and when August came my son was a freshman, in high school. I was a super proud mother because he was my last child to finish school. Chris has always been a people person, and all-around guy. His first years there he made the baseball team, and homecoming court. None of my family came that hurt me and him to the core, but I made sure he enjoyed his night and the activities. He was doing well in academics wise, and he made many friends, which put me. Every weekend we would get in my car, ride, and get lost just to find our way back home.

Doing that helped us learn about the city quickly. Quintion, and TyTy are Monika's children, so they and Chris became very tight. Having family there helped the both of us. Once Chris turned sixteen, he got his first job at Kroger. He was a hard, good, and fast worker. After only two months opening, he was promoted to the front-end manager. He was doing BIG things in Atlanta, and I was super proud of him. A few months later he got his driver's license. His dad got him his first car, a black 1999 ACURA fully loaded. His dad was into buying cars at auctions and fixing them up and reselling them. He hit a sweet lick. Lil Chris drove the wheels off that car literally. I would NEVER ride with him. He should have been a race car driver how fast he drives. Only the young people loved riding with him because I sure didn't.

His sophomore year, he won home-coming two years straight in a row. He always was in a lot of activities during school, he was still doing great in baseball. His dad would come and watch him play sometimes, but always had negative things to say. I thought, he was teaching him how to be a man. Because Lil Chris was defiantly a mother's boy, as the older people would say. His junior year flew by extremely fast, he was almost a grown man, and I was not happy about it. I wasn't ready for him to leave the nest, he was my only son, my protector, my ride or die, even until this day. We are locked tight. I was making good money, living just like I dreamed I would be, and living life.

We finally moved out of our apartment and got a five-bedroom, three full bath home in Douglasville. I dreamed of a house like that when I was young. I would watch TV and see all the nice houses, and always made a mental note that I would own one day. That day had finally come. I was over excited, I was ready to decorate, and was over excited about hosting gatherings, and holidays at my new home. Chris had to change high schools his Senior. That hurt him, but there was no way possible I was going to let him drive almost an hour to his Duluth every day. Too much gas, and too much driving for him. He didn't lose his friends, but he and Endia remain best friends even now.

Endia was from Mississippi as well, but she moved to Georgia before us. I ended up knowing some of the family, because we used to work with them back in Mississippi. Endia and Lil Chris were super tight. She was a well-mannered, high spirited young lady, I absolutely love her. She did her best to keep him in line lol. He started at New Manchester High School, which was right next door to our home. You could literally see the high school through the woods at our home. He met new friends and loved his new school the most.

That Christmas of 2016 I had my first gathering. It was an ugly Christmas sweater party. Monika helped me plan it out. TaShonda, who is Monika's best friend, did all my desserts. We had the regular party food, wings, Rotel dip, sandwiches, meatballs, etc. I order trophies for first, second, and third place. I had a cute FB sign made for the party. My friend Stacee and her husband Nick, my cousin

Doug, and my best friend Wendy all drove to Georgia from Columbus, Mississippi to come party with us. We took pictures, danced, ate, and had a great time. Fellowshipping with friend, co-workers, and family was something I needed because I was dealing with headaches, and health issues that I had not mention to my family at the time.

My health issue took a turn for the worse, the headaches wouldn't stop. They finally did an MRI after months, of meds, and false diagnostics. Finally, got my MRI done, and then my doctor requested a CT scan. A few days later I got a call from the nurse in his office, asking me to come in. I asked, 'is something wrong?' She said, "the doctor would like to discuss the results of your tests with you." I got nervous at first, I wanted to call my mother, but I knew she would call and tell my sister, and all the other family, so I didn't bother. I picked up my phone to text Monika, but I didn't hit send. I'm the type of person that doesn't like people to feel sorry for me, I didn't want sympathy or empathy. I was raised to suck up my hurt, fears, short comings, anything dealing with life, so I went alone.

When the doctor came in the first thing he asked was 'is someone with you?' I said "no" then he let out this big sigh, and said we found lesions on your brain. I had no idea what that meant. He then goes to tell me that they are areas of brain tissue that show damage from injury or disease. He told me they could heal on their own, or they were treatable. But he told me mine were bad. Dr. Hatch then goes on to say, "have you ever had tragic head injuries, or illness?" He then started asking me about the headaches, was I sleeping all the time, was I always tired, and he asked about my eating habits. He then goes to tell me that the brain lesions can be something minor or life-threating. He then told me mines were life-threating because they were so big. He then told me he wanted to run more tests to see if I had MS which is Multiple sclerosis. Which is often seen in people who had it.

We tested it and it came back negative, so this put me into deep thought. I asked him, "could this have happened when I was younger?

"How much younger?" He asked.

"Fourteen."

"Why fourteen?"

"Something happened at that age."

He said in his study he didn't know if it could have happened back that far. He also asked how long I had been dealing with headaches. I told him since I was a teenager but worse as I got older. The reason I asked was because I remember a beating I got as a child. I had disobeyed my father and lied about my whereabouts. He beat me bad that night. I was trying to grab the belt, as he was hitting me, and I ended up having one end, and he had the other. Then next thing I knew somehow, he jerked the belt out my hand, and I fell, and my head hit the bottom of the bed post. I was screaming, and then, I think I blacked out for a few seconds, or something. My dad never stopped beating me at all. After that beating, he made me clean the kitchen. The knot on my head was so big that my eyes started closing.

My mom was at work, so she didn't know at first. I told my father I couldn't see, and my head would not stop hurting. His words to me were take your ass back in that kitchen and finishing cleaning it up. Monique came to help me, but my father made her stop, and told her to go to her room. I finally finished the kitchen and went to our room and went to sleep. I didn't wake up until the next day. I went to use the bathroom, and I looked for my mother. When I walked into the living room she was on the couch on the phone, gossiping lol. She looked at me and asked was I in a fight, I told her no. My dad jumped in and, said "I beat her ass, ask her why?" My mom then went into a rage, she told him, "your ass going to jail. Look at her face. She can't go to school like that they will lock your ass up. That Monday came, and my head was still hurting, my face was swollen, and my head still had the knot just not as big. If you look closely to my left eye, I got a dent in the crack still there until this day.

A few days later the school nurse had called my mom and told her to come pick me up because I was in PE, and I had told the PE teacher my heart was hurting. My mother picked me up because she didn't have to be at work until three. She asked me what the pain felt like, I said it felt like something throbbing inside my head. She took me home gave me two Tylenol and I took a nap. Eventually the headache eased up, but to this day I still deal with headaches.

After the doctor ran all the tests he could run, he then

told me the type of brain lesion I had was called Meningioma brain tumor. He told me tumors are usually not cancerous. Meaning, that unlike cancerous tumors, they don't tend to spread to distant parts of the body. But because of its location, a meningioma can still cause neurological problems. As these tumors grow, they can compress the brain and spinal cord, leading to serious symptoms. He then went to ask if I had experienced changes in vision, such as seeing double or blurriness. Headaches that worsen with time. Hearing loss or ringing in the ears. Memory loss. Loss of smell, Seizures, or weakness in your arms or legs.

When he asked me those questions, everything started to make sense to me. Why I was having the headaches, sleepiness, always tired, moody, back issues just a few to name. I called my best friend Toya to tell her, but when I called, she told me she would call me right back, she was at work when I called. I never got a chance to tell her, because when we talked again, I told her I really didn't want anything. I kept it to myself.

A few weeks later, I had to go in the day before surgery to prep and do blood work. My plans were that when I got home that day, I would tell my son Lil Chris that I had a small procedure. After the blood work was done, I went to Golden Corral to sit down at the buffet to eat. I was sitting there thinking and worrying. I didn't know who to tell or how to tell it without anyone thinking it was it was major, and overreacting. I didn't want them to make me feel worse than I already did. I'm very secretive when it comes to me. I don't like people to worry about me. As I was eating got a call from the nurse asking if I could go to another imaging center the following day. This was the day I was supposed to be having surgery. So, I replied, "Sure, I'll go, but what about my surgery?" She then went to tell me, "The Dr. has seen something, and wants to take another look."

I'm thinking to myself, I'm already stressed, and feel alone about this. Why all these surprises? At this point I wanted to go back home to Mississippi and let another doctor take a look. I felt like I was getting the run around. I also thought that things were worse than he told me previously. I went to the imaging center. The next morning, they ran more tests, and I went home awaiting a call. The next morning, I drove to his clinic and waited in the waiting room for what seemed like forever. They finally called me to the back. I was exhausted from no sleep and had a headache from all this running around. I was sitting in the room and my doctor came in. He sat down and said "Ms. Harris," I said, "its Ledbetter,' we both laughed, and he said, "I just don't know what to say. Since the first MRI your lesion have had some shrinkage."

Keep in mind I had no clue really what that meant, my heart started racing. I felt myself getting mad. He said, "this means, that we can do medication instead of surgery," My eyes got big, and filled with tears one tear dropped and I don't cry. I prayed, I've always prayed, but I felt like I was worthy of this great news. I have fallen short of his comings many times, but he gave me another chance without surgery. I had a sense of relief because for one, no surgery, then I didn't have to tell anyone.

I started on the medication, and then things started to get better, I still dealt with the headaches, but the lesions were still shrinking. My grandmother, my mother, mother, and my mother dealt with headaches all their life, I felt like it was hereditary, because every time they went to the doctor for them, they said they were migraines.

* * *

It was December 2016 Chris first semester as a Senior was almost over and Christmas break, was right around the corner. He and I had a talk about him going to the Air Force. He took the test, and a recruiter came to the house to talk to him. He was short by a few points and was going to take the test again. But it would have to be in January the following year, for some reason. So, we had to have a plan just in case he didn't go to the Air Force. He decided that he wanted to go to college in Alabama. Chris had been an Alabama fan since he was a small child. I told him it was best to move back home for his second semester, and got to EMCC, which is East Mississippi Community College first. He agreed. So, I asked my best friend Toya could he come back to stay with her and graduate, so we wouldn't have to pay out of state tuition. She agreed and my baby was gone in January 2017.

What was I going to do without my baby? He basically did everything for me. So, now it was just me, Dashe and Jordynn, in that big ole house. Things were calmer and quieter since Chris had left lol, everyone knows he's full of energy and the turn up king.

* * *

It was Super Bowl Sunday, February 5, 2017. It was the Falcons vs the New England Patriots. My cousin LaToya is a HUGH fan of the Falcons. And now it was my team because I lived there. I've never been a fan of football. I hosted my first Super Bowl party in my new home. It was the second time the Falcons made it to the playoffs since 1998. My cousins came from both sides, LaToya, Stephanine, Monika, co-workers, family, friends I had a house full. I had all the basic tail gate foods, Rotel, Meatballs, sandwiches, etc. We watched the game, had drinks, and had a good ole time. My uncle snake came he always have me cutting up. The Falcons ended up losing, 34-28. We were devastated. I had a headache from all the screaming and really didn't even know what was going on, lol. All I knew was a touchdown. But the time we all spent together was priceless. As everyone was leaving, I started feeling sad really wasn't ready for them to go, but I knew they had to leave.

* * *

Jordynn 6th birthday was approaching. She wanted to go to Disney World, and I made it happen. Jordynn was back in Mississippi, and Dyiamond. They went to school that Thursday, and I went and picked them up from Mississippi, early at noon, because we had a late flight out that night from Atlanta to Orlando. We got back to my home, packed the car down, and headed to the airport. I had all of Jordynn birthday outfits custom made. People use to tell me "Dee you act like Jordynn your child." I would laugh but I really acted like she was. I even had her bows personalized. I had also got Dy some things. Every trip I took Jordynn on, my GOD baby was going too. We had a late flight that Thursday night at ten o'clock. We boarded the plane, and they were so excited to fly at night. I let them sit by the window so they could see the stars, and the lights below. The look and excitement on their faces let me know I was making them happy. We landed in Orlando Florida that night a little after eleven o'clock. We claimed our luggage and went to the rental car stand to pick up the rental. The reservations were all messed up, it took us about an hour to get things fixed. The girls were exhausted and hungry. We finally got to the resort. I was tired, but the girls were all wired up after I had fed them. They asked to go to the pool because it was still open. I said no, we are about to shower, get some rest so we could get ready for tomorrow. I had purchased a time share, so we were planning to stay there five days. They were on Spring Break of course. The week before the trip I had a bad dream that something bad was about to happen. It bothered me. I always get a feeling right before something happens. I remember my dad told me as a child I had a gift. I never thought about it much more. But it's like I knew it before it happened, I didn't have all the details always right, but I always was point on. So, that night in the room when the kids finally went to sleep, I had a vision, and I immediately began to pray. I picked up the phone and called my son, he didn't answer I texted, and he still didn't answer. When I looked at the time, I figured he was sleeping. I went to sleep with my son so heavy on my mind, because my spirit, vision, and the dream I had, gave me confirmation that someone close to me would die, of tragedy.

In the dream I had, it was my son laying on the ground lifeless, from trying to do a good deed by helping someone. I finally dosed off to sleep to have almost the same exact dream about my son, I knew something was wrong, and my mind had it set that it was my son. When I woke up the next morning which was that Friday, I looked at my phone my son had called and texted me back, I replied and said, "I was just checking on you." He didn't think anything of it because it was normal for me to do check-ups and calls out the blue even if we had just talked. I Never mention my dreams or spirit to him. I got the girls up to get dressed and go get breakfast. We spent the day at the pool, for the most part. That night my sister called me, and she was crying. Naquita is the baby of my mother. My dad had been over to her house, and he had taken sick. I believe he knew how sick he was we just didn't. Dad didn't like staying with anyone. She said he was so weak, and couldn't stand on his own, and that he was about to go to the hospital. I then told her to keep me posted on his condition. It was now Friday night, my sister called and said, "Dee they going to keep him." Me being me and knowing how strong my father was I was like ok and didn't worry too much. The next day I had to go to a time share meeting, for the resort we were in. I had my phone on silent. When I did look at it, I saw that my mom had called, and my sister had called as well, and texted.

She said, "Dee he is doing about the same." My sister is a very strong family person and loves her family. She always feels that family should be first. I'm the total opposite, piss me off I'm done.

Needless to say, we hit the highway and made it to Columbus for safety. I went straight to the hospital to see my dad. I went to the nurse station to get my dad's room number. I walked in and when I looked, I turned around and said to myself, "I'm in the wrong room." I stepped out and looked at the door sign to make sure I was in the right room. It said Charles Ledbetter. I walked back in, and the man lying there didn't look like my dad. His eyes were swollen, almost shut, due to fluid around his eyes. His face looked swollen, not how I pictured he would look, nor was I prepared to see him like that, laying there lifeless. A tear fell, I was in total disbelief. A man lying there that I never seen down, laying there needing help. A strong man that could beat an elephant, in my mind, was just lying there like that was unbearable to look at.

A few minutes after my sister walked in. She sat on the couch with me and filed me in on what was going on. She began to cry, trying to be strong. I told her everything was going to be ok. We then went to handle some things for him. He needed a charger for his phone because we needed to get some information out of there. We went to the southside to grab a few things and went back to the hospital. I went back to my mom's house for the night to get some rest since I had been on the highway all morning, and the hospital basically all that day and night. The next morning, I went to visit dad again. He wasn't doing any better. My mom wasn't feeling good, but she would walk around feeling bad. She wouldn't go to the hospital for herself, but she went with me to visit dad. She had a charger at home that would charge his phone so we could get the information we needed out of it.

Once back at the hospital, she talked to my dad but I'm not sure if he heard her because he didn't move or anything. The meds probably had him out of it. We said our goodbyes and went back to my mom's house. It was Wednesday, my sister called me and said mom was sick and she wanted to go to the doctor. My sister Narquita then told my mom, "If you don't get dressed and go to the emergency room, I'm calling the ambulance. My mom finally got dressed and went to the hospital. When she got to the hospital, I was upstairs on the third floor visiting my dad. I went down to the room where they had my mom. She was lying there waiting for the doctor to return.

Sitting there waiting on all I could think about was my dad laying in that hospital bed upstairs fighting for his life, from the abuse of drugs. As, I was thinking I was getting angry, I HATED every single person that ever sold him any type of drugs. Even family members sold it to him his OWN flesh and blood for money. I would often wonder how they felt knowing they played a part of him lying in that hospital bed, basically lifeless. Dr. Manning finally returned. She gave my mom the results, and my heart dropped to my stomach. They transported her to Tupelo Mississippi hospital, because that was where her heart specialist, main office was. He wanted her closer to him to monitor her condition. I asked her doctor why he let another doctor up her dosage on her medicine. The previous weeks, my mom had gone in to see her doctor, he wasn't available, so his partner was there. She was a nurse practitioner. She put my mother's dosage on her medicine in hopes that would help her feel better. It made things worse. She doubled her dosage on her original medicine, and it was too strong and had dehydrated her kidneys and started shutting them down.

When my mom started crying from the news, she just received all I could reflect on was the night Monique got killed. She had that same hurt look on her face, of hurt, pain, confusion, and anger. But, looking at her she still looked strong, and confident we were going to get through all of this. They took her by ambulance to Tupelo Mississippi, later that Wednesday evening. The next morning, I went to visit her in the hospital in Tupelo. She looked perfectly fine to me on the outside. But, as I reflect, she had the look like she was scared, it was like she wanted to tell me something, but didn't know how.

I was sitting on the couch in her room, looking at cars for my son Chrsitopher because in the next few weeks he would be graduating high school. The plans were to get him a Dodge Charger, fully loaded. He deserved it. He did exactly what he needed to do as a child. I promised him the car of his choice soon as he walked across the stage. He had just lost his grandmother Mildred not even a month before. She was a very bad diabetic. He loved her. She had him so spoiled and gave him anything he wanted.

Knowing that she passed a month before he got to walked across the stage to graduate hurt him badly. Her funeral was on my grandbaby Jordynn birthday April 28, 2017.

The nurse walked in with Morphine to put in my mom's IV. She then goes to say, this is to relax her. I didn't understand at that time honestly nothing made any sense. We started talking and she asked what I was doing. I told her searching for Chris car. Then she said, "Dee cut on cartoons for Jordynn" I said "huh, Jordynn is not here." They wouldn't let children in the rooms there. I was upset at first because Jordynn loved my mother. Then, she says, "Oh, I forgot she's not here, I'm talking out my head again." I looked at her, and asked, "Mom you ok ain't ya?" and, we both laughed. Then she started saying off the wall things, and every time I asked her what in the world she was talking about, she replied with the same answer. "I'm talking out of my head again."

I didn't understand all of that then, but now I do. One of my dad's nurses gave me a pamphlet that said when you're basically in your last days one sign is hallucinations. I left mom and headed back to Columbus to see dad before I went to the house to shower and get some rest.

Dad was still doing the same, his body was rejecting medicine, and basically nothing was working. We watched and let things run their course. Back and forth, back, and forth, daily to see my parents. It was now Monday, May 8, 2017. Dad's doctor said there wasn't anything left for them to do. And, that they were going to put him in hospice. He would still be in hospital and in his same room. That was a relief, so we didn't have to make any arrangements. I knew he was about to go when hospice was the final alternative.

My dad had been on some type of drugs for over forty plus years. It's not a person alive that could have made it that long with the hard drugs my dad used. He was a solider, a hard body is what I called him. I remember once my dad had got so high, he walked down my mom's house, they were separated at the time. He knocked on the door scared, saying that ghost was after him and they were coming to get him. He scared my mom so bad that night. He was walking through her house locking doors, making sure the windows were locked. He honestly thought they were coming to get him. I never knew drugs could do you that bad.

Drugs have ruined so many, people, family, and life in

general. It said that once you are addicted you are always addicted. My dad had multiple strokes and even a heart attack because of drug use. As soon as he was out the hospital, barely can walk or talk, he went straight to get more drugs. I never understood why a person needed drugs so bad. I would lie in a dark room when I had a headache because I didn't want to take anything. My dad ruined it for me. I was so scared to take anything thinking I would get addicted. I didn't want no parts of any drugs, even if it was over the counter at one point in time.

I had to learn to not suffer because I didn't want to pick up a habit of depending on any type of drugs. Drugs change you in so many ways. It clouds your judgement. It destroys families. It even can make you steal and kill that's how strong some drugs are. Drugs are more powerful than life for some.

Now it was Tuesday, May 9, 2017, dad was in the hospice, mom still in the same condition. My aunt Nancy and aunt Mary and a few others went to visit my mom. Later I got a call from the doctor that sent chills over my body. WE HAD TO DECIDE. In my mind my mom was coming home soon, but dad was preparing to leave soon. It was now Wednesday, May 10, 2023, a day I will NEVER IN LIFE FORGET! I was in Jackson when I got the call dad wouldn't make it past the night. When I got to the hospital, he was already gone. I was one hour and three minutes late. I was in disbelief the man I knew as my father all my life was gone, and I was only forty years old. He laid there peacefully. His best friend Donnie had already made me aware that my dad had got right with GOD before he left us.

That wasn't enough for me, I wanted my daddy back. I wanted him to pull through, come home worry me and go to my mom house eating all her snacks up, cracking jokes, making us laugh and telling us lies about how my mom use to be crazy about him lol. But he was gone, and there was nothing I could do about it. We headed to Tupelo the entire ride was tense, and uncomfortable. I didn't know what reaction was about to take place. Getting the news about my mom before leaving my dad's bedside was a responsibility, I wasn't ready for it. I had to inform the family. But we made sure they didn't know until we got there even though some knew anyway. My mom was just lying there like she was asleep. Her eyes were slightly open, like Monique eyes was when she passed. For a split second I seen Monquie, they were in the same position, slightly titled over, and mouth was open just enough to maybe fit a straw.

My mom looked so peaceful. My mom knew she wasn't leaving that hospital. Now that I think back on it, she gave us signs. We just didn't see them. I feel as if she didn't want us to know because it would have been more difficult for us. She was saving us from even more hurt. She got her wish, and her prayer she prayed daily to GOD, and that was to see Tierra and Shan'Qula get grown. Tierra had JUST turned eighteen on April 14, 2017. They both had reached the age to be able to take care of themselves if need be. I learned a valuable lesson behind my parents' death. One, there is power in the tongue. Two, be careful what you pray for, and more importantly, be very clear what you ask for. I feel my mother held on for all of us even though she was tired and wanted to give up so many times. She was strong, resilient, beautiful, and a hard worker when she was able to work. Her job here was done, she did her part plus more.

Planning the funeral arrangements was something I

thought I had to do. For some reason, I felt my parents would have buried me first. I've always felt like I wasn't worthy, and all the wrong I have done I wasn't going to live long. Having to bury a parent is hard, but at the same time is a feeling I can't explain. The numbness, emptiness, the cold feeling I don't wish on anyone. It's how I felt. Even though I had my sister, my children, nieces, nephews, family, and friends I still felt alone. Josh Fenster at the funeral home and a friend helped with the process. Priscilla, Wendy, Drico, Monika, Bubba, just to name a few, had my back so strong. They basically wanted me to relax and try to deal with things the best I could. Things are easier said than done. But we still all try to give words of encouragement, to help make things easier out of kindness.

Carters Funeral Home in Columbus Mississippi, put my parents away so nicely. My mother's favorite color was purple, and my dad's favorite color was gray, where that came from with my dad I have no idea, but I went alone with it lol. Ms. Linda Lang got my mom's attire from Belk's in Columbus. She laid in hat casket like the beautiful queen that she is, she looked like she was in a deep sleep with a slight smile. I knew then she was at peace. My dad laid there looking brave, strong, and confident. That let me know that GOD heard his final prayers and I know he was at peace. My dad let me know he was tired. He was ready to go if the LORD was ready for him. He once told me that he lived his life. He had done everything in life he wanted to do and that he wasn't scared to die, because he was tired. It took me awhile to understand.

"Once you learn the power of the tongue, you will not just say anything." When you learn the power of your thoughts, you won't entertain just anything." And, once you realize the power of your presence. You won't just be anywhere.

After the funeral, I went and sat in the limo. I really didn't want all the hugs, words of encouragement, and the "I'm sorry for your lost." A few people were asking where I was, and I saw my son and a few family members pointing to the limo where I was. One aunt on my dad's side that I didn't get along with too well, approached the limo on the side where I was. I opened the door. I first looked at her, with hate in my eyes. I knew I was wrong, but what she did next really made me want to whip her ass on the church ground. If you know me you know I have no filter and I speak what's on my mind, if not its written all over my face. That's one trait of my daddy that I wish I didn't have. She gave me an envelope. And gave me the fakest hug ever. But, out of respect I hugged her back. We then went to the burial site to say our last goodbyes to my parents for the last time. One of the soldiers walked up to me and placed my dad's flag in my hands, that's when I lost it. They were really gone. LLL "Long Live Laura" and LLC "Long Live Charles"

I'm tired of being strong, I want to be fragile, and the reason why is because, when someone sees someone fragile, they tend to take care of them. Sometimes in life we must go through to get through.

I finally settled after the move back to Mississippi from Atlanta. It was hectic. I had never seen myself moving back home so quickly, my plans were to move back to retire one day. My son walked across the stage to get his diploma; my mind wasn't there it was on my parents. They were supposed to see him walk across that stage. Chris had lost three grandparents within two weeks of each.

That's a burden alone. We go through, just to get through.

Until you are healed, you will damage everything attached to you.
Until you are healed, you will always be who THEY want you to be,
not who you really are.
Until you have healed, you can't help healing no one else.
Until you have healed you will lose focus.
Until you have healed you will not be the best version of you.
Until you have healed, you will stay broken.
You must heal, to be healed.

-Author Deneatrice Ledbetter

Photos
Friends
and
Family

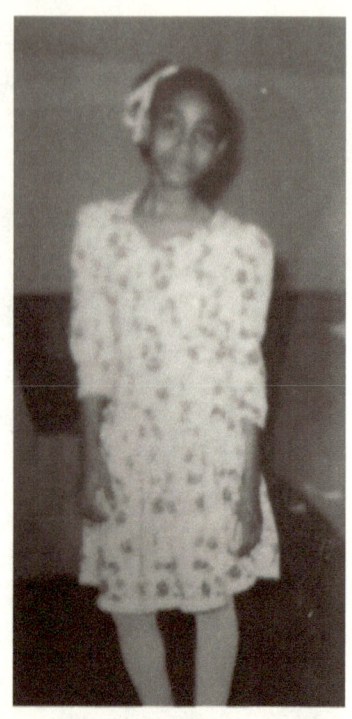

Deneatrice Ledbetter

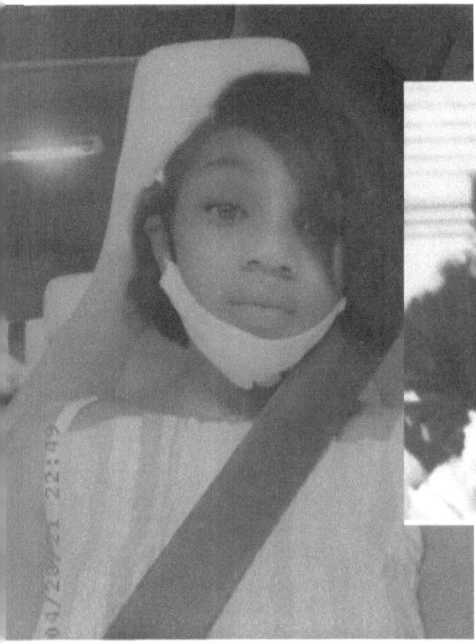

Deneatrice Ledbetter

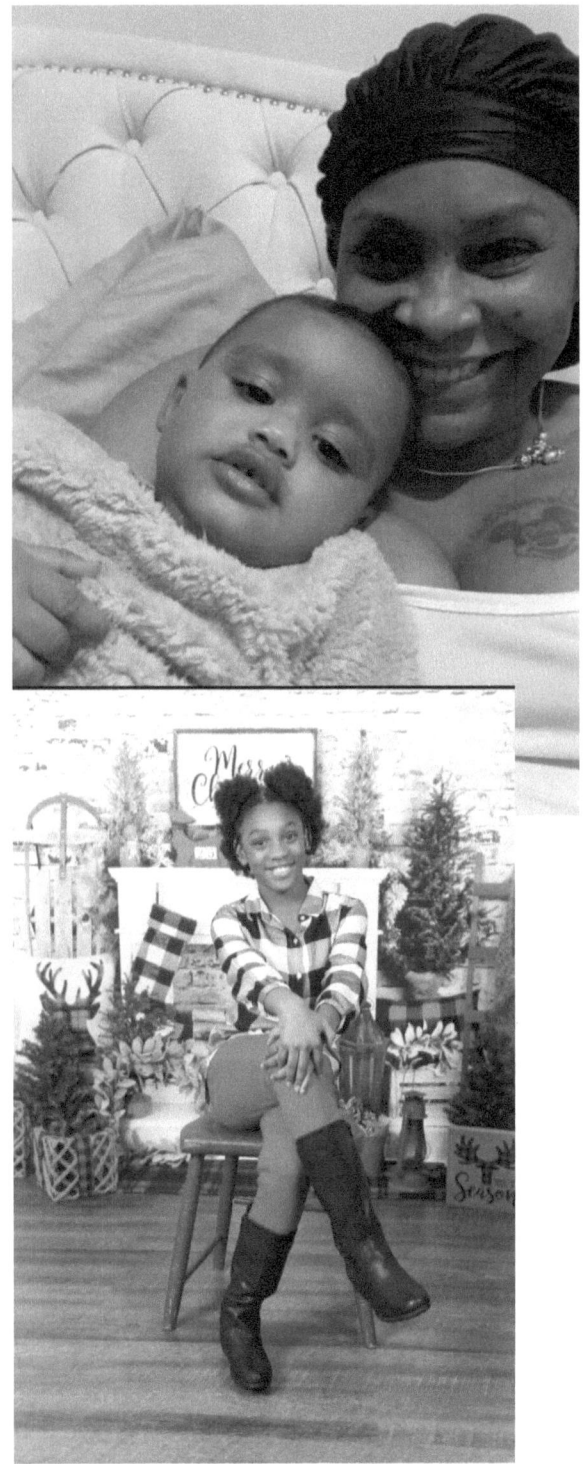

Deneatrice Ledbetter

Little cousins #Honor

Deneatrice Ledbetter

Deneatrice Ledbetter

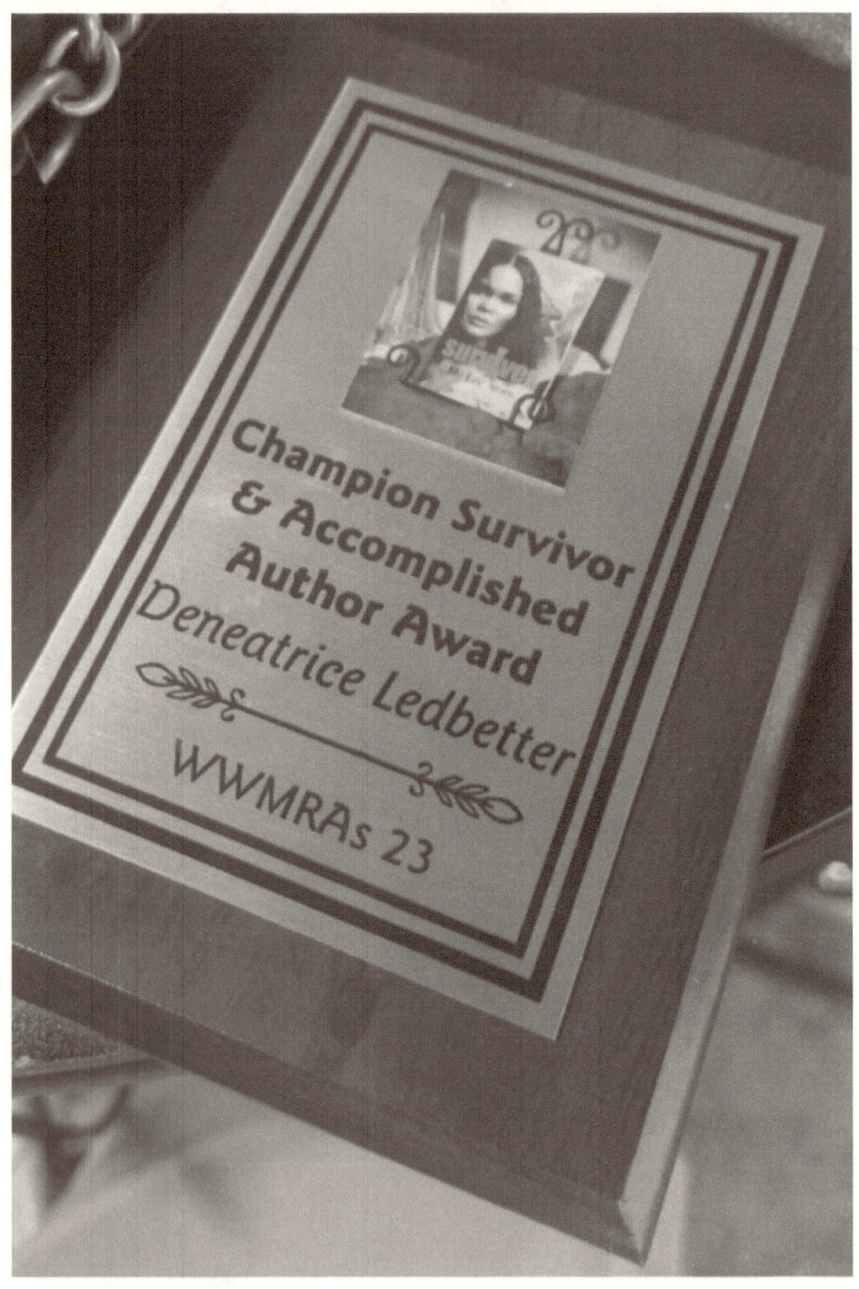

www.ingramcontent.com/pod-product-compliance
Lightning Source LLC
Chambersburg PA
CBHW021635120626
46545CB00002B/554